Step by Step Spreadsheets

GW00493643

Alan Dillon

Gill & Macmillan

Gill & Macmillan Ltd
Hume Avenue
Park West
Dublin 12
with associated companies throughout the world
www.gillmacmillan.ie

0 7171 3487 3

Print origination by Replika Press Pvt. Ltd., India.

The paper used in this book is made from the wood pulp of managed forests.
For every tree felled, at least one tree is planted, thereby renewing natural resources.

A catalogue record is available for this book from the British Library.

Table of Contents

The following symbols are used to indicate chapter objectives, spreadsheet assignments, sections covering spreadsheet theory, rules of correct spreadsheet use, tips and short-cuts and important points.

 Chapter Objectives

 Spreadsheet Theory

 Spreadsheet Assignment

 Tips and Short Cuts

 Important Points

 Spreadsheet Rule

Preface

The assignments in this book were written specifically for Microsoft Excel 2000 but can also be completed using Microsoft Excel for Office XP or Microsoft Excel 97. It is a 'learning through practise' book with lots of practical assignments for the student. No previous knowledge of Excel is needed as the assignments start at a very basic level. The book contains three sections:

- Section 1: Beginners Spreadsheet Assignments
- Section 2: Intermediate and Advanced Spreadsheet Assignments
- Section 3: Project Guidelines and Sample Exams

Students who have no previous spreadsheet experience should start with Section 1. Students already familiar with Microsoft Excel may wish to start with Section 2. However, these students can practise and consolidate existing spreadsheet skills by completing Section 1.

As you progress through the book, assignments gradually become more complex with new spreadsheet topics introduced in each chapter. I would encourage students who are already familiar with the SUM function to complete the assignments contained in Chapter 1, which deals with spreadsheet formulas, as this is a very important area often overlooked by students.

Students who are already familiar with Excel will be able to use this book as an independent study guide. However, as it wasn't possible to include certain details relating to formatting and editing of spreadsheets, I am leaving this to the teacher.

By completing all of the assignments contained in *Step by Step Spreadsheets*, you will have covered all the necessary course material required to successfully complete the FETAC (NCVA) Level 2 Spreadsheet Methods Module.

New versions of Microsoft Excel will be introduced over time. Because the assignments deal more with the principles of spreadsheets than with the features of Microsoft Excel, I am confident that, except for a few minor inconsistencies, they will also be compatible with future versions of Microsoft Excel.

Thanks to my students for giving me the inspiration and energy to write this book.

Alan Dillon
January 2003

LECTURERS!
SUPPORT MATERIAL

For your support material check our website at:

www.gillmacmillan.ie

Support material is available to lecturers only within a secure area of this website.

Support material for this book consists of solutions to assignments or tasks.

To access support material for *Step by Step Spreadsheets*:

1. Go to www.gillmacmillan.ie
2. Click on the 'logon' button and enter your username and password.
   (If you do not already have a username and password you must register. To do this click the 'register' button and complete the online registration form. Your username and password will then be sent to you by email.)
3. Click on the link 'Support Material'.
4. Select the title *Step by Step Spreadsheets*.

Introduction

 The spreadsheet was invented in 1978 by Dan Bricklen who, at the time, was a business student attending university in America. As Dan attended lectures in finance, he found that his teachers had to constantly rub out and rewrite the board as a change in one number, e.g. an interest rate or a tax rate, would affect many other numbers. The solution was Visicalc, the first computerised spreadsheet. In the spreadsheet the effects of a change in one number could be seen instantly. Visicalc was quickly overtaken by Lotus 1-2-3, which became the leading spreadsheet package in the 1980s. Since the early 1990s, Excel has been the most popular spreadsheet.

What is a Spreadsheet?

A spreadsheet is made up of rows and columns. Each row is identified by a unique number (1, 2, 3 and so on). Each column is identified by a unique letter (A, B, C and so on). The intersection of a row and a column is called a cell. The current cell is indicated by the cell pointer.

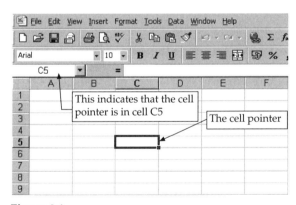

Figure 0.1

In Figure 0.1, the cell pointer is in column C and row 5. This cell is called C5.

What Can a Spreadsheet Do For You?

If you work with numbers regularly then a spreadsheet may save you lots of time.

Spreadsheets are great for all types of financial calculations such as budgets, cash-flow statements, profit and loss accounts and travel expenses. They can also be used for statistical analysis by using special functions to calculate averages and standard deviations. Spreadsheets can help you present information in a way that is easy to understand by using a wide range of graphs.

Working with Spreadsheets

A spreadsheet offers the user a variety of tools that speed up tasks such as formatting, moving, copying and printing data. These tools can be accessed through the menu or the toolbars.

The Menu

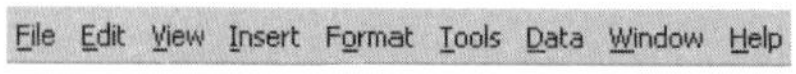

File Edit View Insert Format Tools Data Window Help

Figure 0.2

Each section of the menu can be accessed by moving the mouse pointer over the menu name and clicking with the left button or by holding down ALT on the keyboard and typing the letter which is underlined, e.g. ALT and F will access the File menu, Alt and E will access the Edit menu, and so on.

The menu is divided into nine sections, each of which offers different functions to the user. The sections of the menu may be summarised as follows:

1. **File**: Contains basic tools for working with spreadsheet files – open, close, save and print files, change page set-up and exit from the spreadsheet package.
2. **Edit**: Contains basic tools for rearranging data in a document – moving, copying and deleting – and also allows the user to search for and replace specific data.
3. **View**: This can be used to insert headers and footers, zoom in on particular areas of the spreadsheet and customise menus and toolbars.
4. **Insert**: Allows the user to insert additional rows and columns as well as graphs, pictures and links to other files or websites on the Internet.
5. **Format**: This section of the menu can be used to change the appearance of data in the spreadsheet by using different font styles, sizes and colours as well as borders and shading.
6. **Tools**: The Tools menu can be used to check spelling, protect areas of the spreadsheet and create macros.
7. **Data**: The Data menu allows the user to sort spreadsheet data and to carry out statistical analysis on spreadsheet data.
8. **Window**: The Window menu allows the user to switch between spreadsheets when more than one spreadsheet is open and to display multiple spreadsheets simultaneously.
9. **Help**: This section provides assistance to the user through tutorials and an index where the user can search for help on specific topics.

The Formatting Toolbar

Using buttons on the formatting toolbar is a quick and easy way of changing the appearance of your spreadsheet. To use a button on the formatting toolbar, move the mouse pointer above the button and click once with the left button.

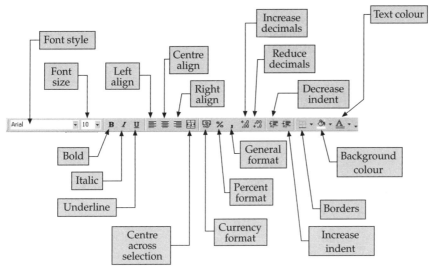

Figure 0.3

The Standard Toolbar

The buttons on the standard toolbar allow the user to quickly open, save and create new documents, move and copy data, work with graphics, sort spreadsheet data and print spreadsheets. To use a button on the standard toolbar, move the mouse pointer above the button and click once with the left button.

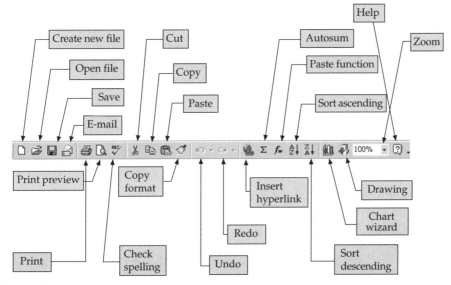

Figure 0.4

The Formula Bar

The formula bar appears just below the standard toolbar. It provides us with two important pieces of information: the current location of the cell pointer and the contents of the current cell. A cell may contain text, a number or a formula/function.

When a cell contains a formula, as shown in Figure 0.6, the result of the formula is displayed in the cell and the formula is displayed in the formula bar. The formula bar is also used for editing individual cell data.

| The current cell is A1 | The number 724.6 is currently in cell A1 |

A1   ▾   = 724.6

Figure 0.5

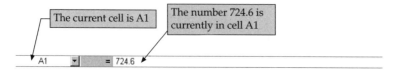

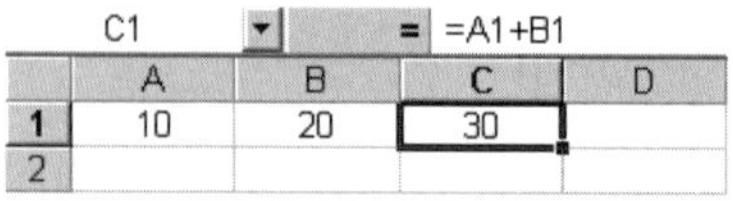

Figure 0.6

The Spreadsheet Window

The spreadsheet window displays cells where the user can type data. Because a spreadsheet is too large to fit on one screen, the spreadsheet window can only display a small portion of the entire spreadsheet at any given time.

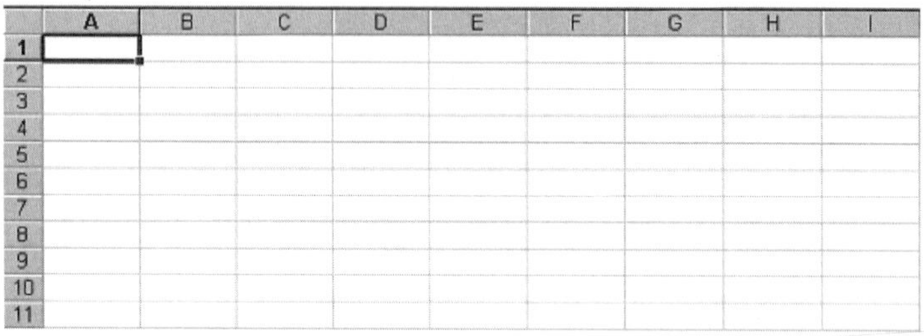

Figure 0.7

The Worksheet Tabs

Each spreadsheet workbook is divided into a number of worksheets. Information can be entered on many worksheets and the worksheets can be linked. For example, Sheet1 could contain data relating to the sales department, Sheet2 could contain data relating to the production department and Sheet3 could contain data relating to the total costs and revenues of both production and sales. The worksheet tabs can be used to move from worksheet to worksheet. In Figure 0.8, the user is currently in Sheet1.

Figure 0.8

Mouse Pointers

The shape of the mouse pointer determines what will happen when you click the left or right button of the mouse and also determines what will happen when you click and drag with the left mouse button.

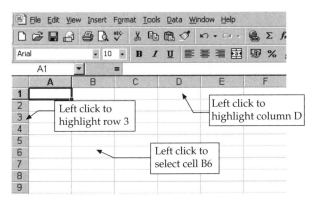

Figure 0.9

Mouse Pointer for Selecting Cells, Rows or Columns

As shown above in Figure 0.10, the mouse pointer takes the shape of a white cross when you point at any cell within the spreadsheet and also when you point at column letters and row numbers. With this mouse pointer, a single left click will select a cell. Clicking the left mouse button and dragging will select a range of cells. This mouse pointer will also select an entire row by clicking a particular row number and will select an entire column by clicking a particular column letter.

Figure 0.10

Mouse Pointer for Selecting Menu Items and Toolbar Buttons and for Moving Data

As shown in Figure 0.12, the mouse pointer takes the shape of a white arrow pointing diagonally upwards to the left when you point at a menu name such as File or Edit and when you point at toolbar buttons. The mouse pointer will also take this shape when you point at the edge of the cell pointer. With this mouse pointer, a single left click will select a menu item or a toolbar button. This mouse pointer will also move data by pointing at the edge of the cell pointer or highlighted area, holding down the left mouse button and dragging to the new location.

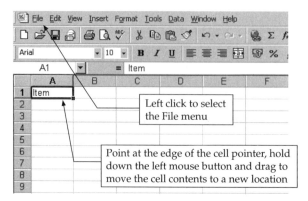

Figure 0.11

Figure 0.12

Mouse Pointer for Copying the Contents of the Current Cell Downwards or to the Right

The mouse pointer takes the shape of a black cross, as shown in Figure 0.14, when you point at the black dot, called the fill handle, at the bottom right corner of the cell pointer. With this mouse pointer, holding down the left button and dragging will copy the cell contents.

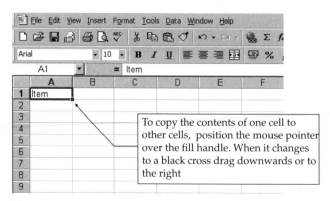

Figure 0.13

Figure 0.14

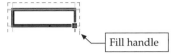

Figure 0.15

Mouse Pointer for Adjusting Row Height

The mouse pointer takes the shape in Figure 0.17 when you point at the dividing line above or below a row number. With this mouse pointer, holding down the left button and dragging upwards will decrease row height. Dragging downwards will increase row height.

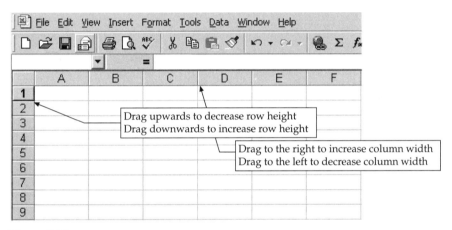

Figure 0.16

Figure 0.17

Mouse Pointer for Adjusting Column Width

The mouse pointer takes the shape in Figure 0.18 when you point at the dividing line to the left or right of a column letter. Drag the mouse pointer to the left to decrease column width or to the right to increase column width.

Figure 0.18

Summary of Mouse Pointers

Table 0.1

Mouse Pointer	Function
✥ Figure 0.10	• Selecting cells, rows or columns
▨ Figure 0.12	• Selecting menu items and toolbar buttons • Moving cell data
✚ Figure 0.14	• Copying cell data
╪ Figure 0.17	• Adjusting row height
╫ Figure 0.18	• Adjusting column width

Entering Data in a Spreadsheet

One item of data is entered in each spreadsheet cell. An item of data can be text, a number, a formula or a function.

Once you type something in a cell, Figure 0.19 will appear above the column headings.

Figure 0.19

In Figure 0.20, the cell pointer is in A1 and the user has typed the text 'Month'. This text can be entered in the spreadsheet in one of two ways: either by pressing Enter on the keyboard or by clicking the green correct symbol with the left mouse button. To reject what was typed press Esc on the keyboard or click the red X with the left mouse button.

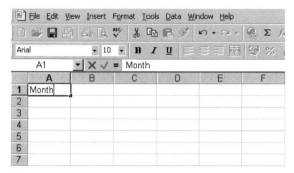

Figure 0.20

What Can You Type in a Spreadsheet Cell?

Depending on what you type in a spreadsheet cell, it will be interpreted as one of three things: a number, text or a formula/function.

A Number

This is anything that begins with a number and doesn't contain any text.

Examples: 3
              33
              156
But not: 3 cars
              33x
              room 156

Text

This is anything that begins with a letter or a symbol, or contains a letter or a symbol and doesn't begin with the equal sign.

Examples: Monday
              87D5672
              10CF

A Formula/Function

This is anything that begins with the equal sign and contains cell references or function names.

Examples: =A1–A2
               =max(B15:B30)
               =C32*C33-A10

Formulas will be explained in detail in Chapter 1. Functions will be introduced in Chapter 2.

Beginners Spreadsheet Assignments

Chapter 1: Spreadsheet Formulas

- Enter data in a spreadsheet
- Print a spreadsheet
- Create basic spreadsheet formulas using addition, subtraction, multiplication and division
- Move and copy data
- Use brackets in a formula
- Use absolute cell references
- Calculate percentages.

Chapter 2: Spreadsheet Functions

- Assign a name to a single cell
- Assign a name to a range of cells
- Use the SUM, AVERAGE, MAX, MIN, COUNT and COUNTA functions
- Use advanced functions: POWER, SQRT, DB, SUMIF and COUNTIF.

Chapter 3: Naming and Linking Worksheets

- Name and copy worksheets
- Create formulas to read data from multiple worksheets
- Create formulas linked to cells in multiple worksheets.

Chapter 4: Spreadsheet Charts

- Create column charts, bar charts, line charts, pie charts and XY charts
- Modify existing charts to include new data.

Chapter 5: Sorting Spreadsheet Data

- Sort spreadsheet data in ascending and descending order
- Use a custom sort for weekdays and month names
- Create you own custom sort.

Progress Test 1

1

Spreadsheet Formulas

In Chapter 1, you will learn how to

- Enter data in a spreadsheet
- Print a spreadsheet
- Create basic spreadsheet formulas using addition, subtraction, multiplication and division
- Move and copy data
- Use brackets in a formula
- Use absolute cell references
- Calculate percentages.

Creating a Spreadsheet Formula

In the following example, we'll create a formula that calculates the total tickets sold. There is no need to enter the data in a spreadsheet. For the moment we'll just write out the formula.

Table 1.1

	A	B
1		**Tickets Sold**
2	Peter	21
3	Rose	38
4	Mark	32
5	Total	

Creating a Spreadsheet Formula to Calculate Total Tickets Sold

To create the formula correctly follow these three steps:

1. Write down the formula in numbers: **21 + 38 + 32**
2. Change the numbers to cell references: **B2 + B3 + B4**
3. Put = in front of the formula created in step two above: **= B2 + B3 + B4**.

If you were entering this formula in the above spreadsheet, you would move the cell pointer to B5 and then type = B2 + B3 + B4.

 Tip: Many students make mistakes when creating formulas because they don't follow these three steps.

For each assignment in Chapter 1, create your formulas by writing out the three steps on paper before typing the formula in the spreadsheet. When you get used to this method of creating formulas you'll find that you can do this exercise mentally without writing it down. However, if you're having difficulty creating a formula, always revert to the three steps.

How Do I Start Using Excel?

To start Excel double click the Excel icon on the desktop, as shown below.

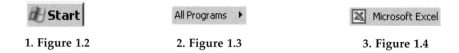

Figure 1.1

Alternatively, click the Start button, select Programs or All Programs and then select Microsoft Excel.

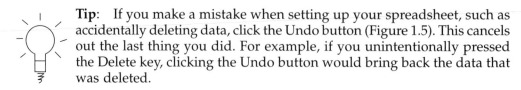

1. **Figure 1.2**   2. **Figure 1.3**   3. **Figure 1.4**

Spreadsheet Formulas Assignment One

Start Excel by using one of the methods outlined above. A new spreadsheet workbook is then displayed. Enter data as shown in Table 1.2. Enter addition formulas in the shaded cells to complete the spreadsheet.

Tip: If you make a mistake when setting up your spreadsheet, such as accidentally deleting data, click the Undo button (Figure 1.5). This cancels out the last thing you did. For example, if you unintentionally pressed the Delete key, clicking the Undo button would bring back the data that was deleted.

1. Using the three steps for creating a formula, calculate the total sales per day.

Undo button

Figure 1.5

Table 1.2

	A	B	C	D	E
1	Ticket Sales				
2		Ocean's Eleven	Monsters, Inc.	The Lord of The Rings	**Total**
3	Monday	250	185	205	
4	Tuesday	290	190	210	
5	Wednesday	300	120	220	
6	Thursday	260	200	188	
7	Friday	450	208	180	
8					
9	Total				

2. Copy this formula using fill down (*with the answer to your first formula displayed in the cell pointer, position the mouse pointer over the fill handle. When the mouse pointer changes to a black cross, drag downwards to copy the formula*).

Figure 1.6

3. Create a formula to calculate the total sales per film.
4. Copy this formula using fill right.

Figure 1.7

5. Increase the width of column A.

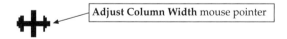

Figure 1.8

6. Centre the data in columns B, C, D and E using the center button.

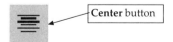

Figure 1.9

7. Click the bold button to format the headings to bold, as shown in Table 1.2.

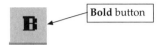

Figure 1.10

8. Click the Save button and save the spreadsheet as **Cinema Ticket Sales**.

Figure 1.11

 ## Moving Data in a Spreadsheet (Cut and Paste)

Moving data from one location to another in a spreadsheet requires three steps.

1. Highlight the data to be moved either by using the mouse or by pressing F8, followed by an arrow key. Data can also be highlighted by pressing an arrow key while holding down the Shift key.

2. Click the Cut button on the toolbar (or select Cut from the Edit menu). This copies the highlighted data from its current location and places it in a temporary storage area referred to as the Clipboard.

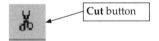

Figure 1.12

3. Position the cell pointer in the new location for the data and click the Paste button (or select Paste from the Edit menu). This copies the contents of the Clipboard to the new location and erases the data from its original location.

Figure 1.13

Copying Data in a Spreadsheet (Copy and Paste)

Copying data from one location to another in a spreadsheet also requires three steps.

1. Highlight the data to be copied using any of the three methods already described.

2. Click the Copy button on the toolbar (or select Copy from the Edit menu). This copies the highlighted data from its current location and places it in a temporary storage area referred to as the Clipboard.

Copy button

Figure 1.14

3. Position the cell pointer in the new location for the data and click the Paste button (or select Paste from the Edit menu). This copies the contents of the Clipboard to the new location.

Paste button

Figure 1.15

 Spreadsheet Formulas Assignment Two

Click the New button to create a new spreadsheet workbook and enter data as shown in Table 1.3 on page 8. Enter multiplication and addition formulas in the shaded cells to complete the spreadsheet.

New button

Figure 1.16

1. Calculate total cost. Copy this formula using fill down.

Fill Down mouse pointer

Figure 1.17

2. Calculate subtotal, VAT and total.
3. Move the heading Invoice to E1. (*Use the cut and paste buttons.*)

Cut button   Paste button

Figure 1.18   **Figure 1.19**

Table 1.3

	A	B	C	D	E
1	Computer Accessories			Invoice	
2					
3	Item	Quantity	Unit Price		Total Cost
4	2HD Disketters	100	0.9		
5	Anti Glare Guard	5	25		
6	Screen Cleaner	20	1		
7	CD Rack	8	7.5		
8	Screen Wipes	100	0.2		
9	Compressed Air	2	10		
10	Disk Labels	50	0.1		
11					
12				Subtotal	
13				VAT@21%	
14				Total	

4. Use the Currency button to format all money amounts to currency.

Currency button

Figure 1.20

Tip: If a number changes to ##### when you format to currency, this means you need to increase the column width.

5. Increase the width of column A.

Adjust Column Width mouse pointer

Figure 1.21

6. Centre the data in columns B, C and E.

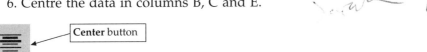

Center button

Figure 1.22

7. Save the spreadsheet as **Computer Accessories Invoice**.

Save button

Figure 1.23

Rule: Always use the formatting toolbar to insert a euro sign. Typing a euro sign can cause Excel to interpret the cell entry as text, leading to errors in formulas, e.g. type 34.5 and format to currency to get €34.50.

Spreadsheet Formulas Assignment Three

Create a new spreadsheet workbook and enter data as shown in Table 1.4. Enter multiplication, addition and subtraction formulas in the shaded cells to complete the spreadsheet.

Table 1.4

	A	B	C	D	E	F	G
1	Income	Class Size	Course Fee	Total Fees	Number of Classes	Duration of Class	Total Hours
2	Spreadsheets	25	80		15	2	
3	Database	20	100		20	2	
4	Word Processing	30	65		12	1.5	
5							
6	Expenditure	Hourly Rate	Total Wages	Profit			
7	Spreadsheets	17.5					
8	Database	19.5					
9	Word Processing	16.5					

Tip: To wrap text within a cell select **Format** followed by **Cells** from the menu. Now click the **Alignment** tab and select 'Wrap text'.

1. Calculate the total fees (class size multiplied by course fee).
2. Calculate total hours (number of classes multiplied by duration of class).

3. Calculate the total wages (hourly rate multiplied by the total hours for each course).
4. Calculate the profit (total fees minus total wages for each course).
5. Copy all formulas using fill down.
6. Format all money amounts to currency.

Figure 1.24

7. Format headings to bold, as shown.

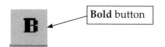

Figure 1.25

8. Adjust column widths to display data, as shown.
9. Centre the data in columns B to G.

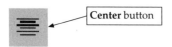

Figure 1.26

10. Use the decrease decimals button to adjust the course fee amounts to zero decimal places.

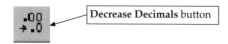

Figure 1.27

11. Save the spreadsheet as **Evening Classes Budget**.

Using Division in a Spreadsheet Formula

Rule: In any formula that doesn't contain brackets, multiplication and division are always done first.

Example: Using Brackets to Change the Natural Order of a Formula
In order to calculate average daily attendance in the spreadsheet displayed in Table 1.5 on page 11, we must first add the attendance for Monday to Friday and then divide by five. Brackets are required to force the spreadsheet to add before it divides. The correct formula is = (B4 + B5 + B6 + B7 + B8)/5.

If this formula was entered without brackets as = B4 + B5 + B6 + B7 + B8/5, then B8/5 (division) would be carried out first giving 110, which would then be added to the remaining four numbers resulting in 2512.

Rule: To change the natural order of a formula, use brackets. Whatever is enclosed in brackets will be calculated first.

Table 1.5

	A	B
1	College Attendance	
2		
3		No. of Students
4	Monday	583
5	Tuesday	601
6	Wednesday	610
7	Thursday	608
8	Friday	550
9		
10		
11	**Average Daily Attendance**	**= (B4 + B5 + B6 + B7 + B8)/5 equals 590.4**

Spreadsheet Formulas Assignment Four

Create a new spreadsheet workbook and enter data as shown in Table 1.6 on page 12. Enter formulas in the shaded cells to complete the spreadsheet.

Tip: Day and month names can be copied using the fill handle. Move the cell pointer to the first day or month name. Position the mouse pointer over the fill handle at the bottom right corner of the cell pointer. When the mouse pointer changes to a black cross, drag downwards or to the right to copy. The day or month names will adjust as they are copied.

1. Increase the width of column A.
2. Using the three steps for creating a formula, calculate the average daily sales for fruit. Copy this formula using fill right.

Note: *The correct answer is 92.5. If the addition is not enclosed in brackets, the answer will be 513.33.*

Table 1.6

	A	B	C	D	E
1	Sales Analysis				
2					
3		Fruit	Drink	Hardware	Dairy
4	Monday	100	20	15	150
5	Tuesday	95	15	10	125
6	Wednesday	80	18	8	140
7	Thursday	120	10	12	150
8	Friday	110	50	14	180
9	Saturday	50	70	20	70
10					
11	Average Daily Sales				

3. Use the increase and decrease decimals buttons so that all averages are displayed with two decimal places.

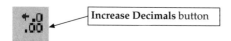 Increase Decimals button

Figure 1.28

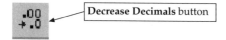 Decrease Decimals button

Figure 1.29

4. Format headings to bold, as shown.
5. Centre data, as shown.
6. Save the spreadsheet as **Sales Analysis**.

 Spreadsheet Formulas Assignment Five

Open the Cinema Ticket Sales spreadsheet. Enter division formulas in the shaded cells to complete the spreadsheet.

1. Insert an extra row and column, as shown in Table 1.7.
2. Calculate the average ticket sales by film and by day.
3. Copy all formulas using fill down and fill right.
4. Use the decrease decimals button so that all averages display no decimal places.

Table 1.7

	A	B	C	D	E	F
1	Ticket Sales					
2		Ocean's Eleven	Monsters, Inc.	The Lord of the Rings	Total	Average
3	Monday	250	185	205	640	
4	Tuesday	290	190	210	690	
5	Wednesday	300	120	220	640	
6	Thursday	260	200	188	648	
7	Friday	450	208	180	838	
8						
9	Total	1550	903	1003		
10	Average					

5. Format headings to bold, as shown.
6. Centre the data, as shown.
7. Click the Save button to save the changes.

How a Spreadsheet Works with Percentages

A percentage is a method of expressing a fraction in relation to the number 100, e.g. $^1/_4$ is 25% and $^3/_4$ is 75%. To convert a fraction to a percentage, we multiply by 100, e.g. $^1/_4 \times 100 = 100/4 = 25\%$, or $^3/_4 \times 100 = 300/4 = 75\%$.

In a spreadsheet there is no need to multiply by 100. The spreadsheet does this for you when you click the Percent Style button on the toolbar.

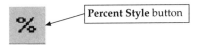

Percent Style button

Figure 1.30

Percentages Example
Type in 0.25, then click the Percent Style button to get 25%.
Type in 0.4, then click the Percent Style button to get 40%.

Rule: To get a percentage between 0 and 100 when you click the Percent Style button, the number in the cell must be between zero and one. Percentages can also be entered directly without using the percentage button. Entering 25% in a cell achieves the same result as entering 0.25 and then clicking the Percent Style button.

Printing a Spreadsheet

It's a good idea to get a preview of what your spreadsheet will look like on a printed page before you actually print it. Previewing the spreadsheet allows you to see if you need to make any adjustments, such as reducing the width of some columns so that the spreadsheet fits on the page. Sometimes you may have to change the page orientation to landscape if the spreadsheet is too wide to fit on a page in portrait orientation.

To preview how the spreadsheet will appear on a printed page click the Print Preview button.

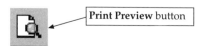

Figure 1.31

Once you're in Print Preview, you can make some useful adjustments to your printout by clicking the Setup button. When you click the Setup button, the Page Setup dialog box is displayed, as shown in Figure 1.33.

Figure 1.32

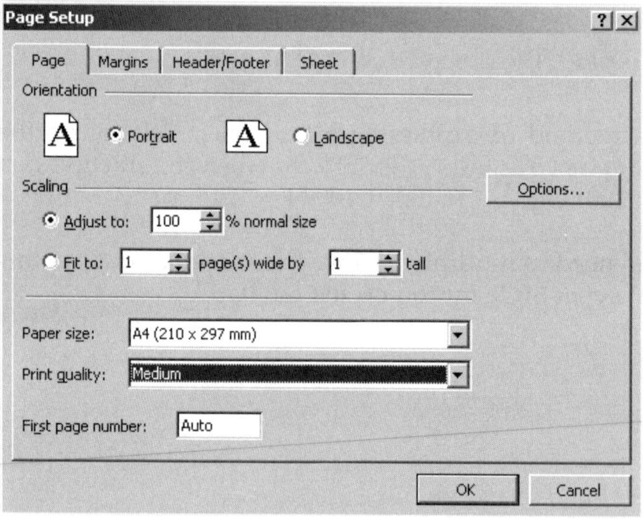

Figure 1.33

The Page Setup dialog box has four sections, which can be used as follows.

1. Select the **Page** tab if you want to change the orientation of the printed spreadsheet from portrait to landscape. You can also shrink your spreadsheet onto one page by specifying a percentage less than 100% of the normal size. The downside of this is that the print will be smaller.

2. Select the **Margins** tab if you want to adjust the size of one or more of the page margins.

3. Select the **Header/Footer** tab if you want to include headers and footers in the printed spreadsheet.

4. Select the **Sheet** tab if you want to print the gridlines and the row and column headings.

To print your spreadsheet without previewing it, simply click the Print button.

Figure 1.34

 Tip: If you only want to print a section of your spreadsheet, highlight the range of cells containing the data you want to print. Select **File** followed by **Print**, and click **Selection** in the 'Print What' section of the Print dialog box.

 Spreadsheet Formulas Assignment Six

Create a new spreadsheet workbook and enter data as shown in Table 1.8. Enter formulas in the shaded cells to complete the spreadsheet.

Table 1.8

	A	B	C	D	E	F
1	Household Budget					
2						
3		January	February	March	April	May
4	Opening Balance	55				
5	Interest Rate	.03	.031	.03	.029	.029
6						
7	Income					
8						
9	Deposit Interest					
10	Children's Allowance	50	50	50	50	50
11	Wages	502.5	502.5	502.5	502.5	502.5
12	Grinds	60	60	90	60	30
13	Night Classes	71.3	71.3	71.3	71.3	71.3

(Contd.)

Table 1.8 *(Contd.)*

	A	B	C	D	E	F
14	Rent	355	355	355	355	355
15						
16	**Total Income**					
17						
18	**Expenses**					
19						
20	Mortgage	618.26	618.26	618.26	618.26	618.26
21	Petrol	43.8	40.9	38.73	39.5	32.09
22	Food	65.5	59.91	72.65	69.77	83.46
23	Car Insurance	65.7	65.7	65.7	65.7	65.7
24	Car Tax					218
25	Tuition Fees	90			110	
26						
27	**Total Expenses**					
28						
29	**Closing Balance**					

Tip: It's a good idea to save your spreadsheet before you complete it and then click the Save button every ten minutes or so. If you get into the habit of doing this you won't lose hours of work if there's a power cut or if you accidentally close your spreadsheet without saving it.

Tip: When the spreadsheet is too big to fit in the spreadsheet window, lock the headings in place with Freeze Panes. Position the cell pointer in B4 in this case and then select **Window** followed by **Freeze Panes** from the menu.

1. Using the Percent Style button format all interest rates to percentage, one decimal place.

Percent Style button

Figure 1.35

2. Calculate monthly deposit interest (opening balance multiplied by the interest rate).

3. Calculate total income and total expenses.

4. Calculate the closing balance.

5. The opening balance for February is the closing balance for January (*the formula for February's opening balance is = B29*).

6. Copy all formulas using fill right. (**Note**: *the deposit interest and opening balances for March, April and May will be 0 until you copy the closing balance formula across.*)

7. Using the Print Preview button, preview how your spreadsheet will look when printed.

Print Preview button

Figure 1.36

8. Format all money amounts to currency.
9. Format headings to bold, as shown.
10. Centre the data in columns B to F.
11. Print the spreadsheet using the Print button.
12. Save the spreadsheet as **Household Budget**.

Absolute and Relative Cell References

Spreadsheet formulas refer to cells. Each reference a formula makes to a cell can be relative or absolute. So far we have only used relative cell references in formulas.

Relative cell references change when a formula is moved or copied to other cells. For example, the formula = A2 + A3 will become = B2 + B3 when it's copied one column to the right.

Absolute cell references don't change when a formula is moved or copied to other cells. Cell references can be made absolute by typing $ on either side of the column letter. Without the dollar signs cell references are relative.

Examples of Relative and Absolute Cell References

Relative	*Absolute*
B1	$B$1
A10	$A$10
D15	$D$15

In the following example, we'll see when absolute cell references are needed and what happens when formulas containing absolute and relative cell references are copied.

Using Absolute and Relative Cell References in a Formula

In Table 1.9, the formula is incorrect when copied down because the reference to B1 changes to B2, B3, B4, B5, B6 and B7 instead of remaining as B1 for all formulas. To prevent the reference to B1 from changing we need to make it absolute by typing $ on either side of the letter B, giving = B4*$B$1. When this formula is copied, the reference to B1 doesn't change, as shown in Table 1.10.

Table 1.9

	A	B	C	
1	VAT Rate	20%		Because this formula contains relative cell references, both cell references change each time the formula is copied down to the next row. This is correct for the part of the formula that refers to the Cost but incorrect for the part of the formula that refers to VAT rate
2				
3	Product	Cost	VAT	
4	DVD Player	220	=B4***B1**	
5	Digital Camera	361	=B5***B2**	
6	Fax Machine	158	=B6***B3**	
7	Personal Stereo	55	=B7***B4**	
8	Portable Radio	10	=B8***B5**	
9	Clock Radio	25	=B9***B6**	
10	Mini Disc System	140	=B10***B7**	

Adjusted Formulas with Absolute Cell References

Table 1.10

	A	B	C
1	VAT Rate	20%	
2			
3	Product	Cost	VAT
4	DVD Player	220	=B4***$B$1**
5	Digital Camera	361	=B5***$B$1**
6	Fax Machine	158	=B6***$B$1**
7	Personal Stereo	55	=B7***$B$1**
8	Portable Radio	10	=B8***$B$1**
9	Clock Radio	25	=B9***$B$1**
10	Mini Disc System	140	=B10***$B$1**

Tip: Highlighting a cell reference in a formula and pressing F4 converts from relative to absolute.

Spreadsheet Formulas Assignment Seven

Create a new spreadsheet workbook and enter data as shown in Table 1.11. Enter formulas in the shaded cells to complete the spreadsheet, using absolute cell references where appropriate.

Table 1.11

	A	B	C	D	E	F
1	PAYE Rate	0.2	PRSI Rate	0.035		
2						
3	Employee Name	Gross Pay	PAYE	PRSI	Total	Net Pay
4	John O Neill	301.04				
5	Mary Doyle	253.77				
6	Peter Hennessy	267.43				
7	Sinead Murray	195.83				
8	Noreen Keogh	155.98				
9	Susan Donovan	266.22				
10	Tom Larkin	180.01				

1. Format the PAYE rate to percentage, zero decimal places and the PRSI rate to percentage, one decimal place.
2. Calculate PAYE.
3. Calculate PRSI.
4. Calculate the total by adding PAYE and PRSI.
5. Net pay is gross pay minus total.
6. Copy all formulas using fill down.
7. Format all money amounts to currency.
8. Format all headings to bold.
9. Adjust column widths where necessary.
10. Centre the data in cells B3 to F10.
11. Print the spreadsheet.
12. Save the spreadsheet as **Weekly Payroll**.

Spreadsheet Formulas Assignment Eight

Create a new spreadsheet workbook and enter data as shown in Table 1.12. Enter formulas in the shaded cells to complete the spreadsheet.

Table 1.12

	A	B	C	D	E	F	G
1				VAT	0.21		
2							
3	Car Type	Daily Rate	Days Hired	Discount	Subtotal	VAT	Total
4	Fiesta	40	5	10			
5	Primera	45.5	2	5			
6	Sunny	42	1	2.5			
7	Escort	42	3	7.5			
8	Corsa	39.5	7	15			
9	Tigra	50	10	25			
10	Corolla	42	14	30			
11	Focus	42	7	16.5			
12	Ibiza	40	5	10			

1. Format the VAT rate to percentage, zero decimal places.
2. Calculate the subtotal (daily rate multiplied by the days hired minus the discount). *Remember that multiplication is always done before subtraction in any formula that doesn't contain brackets.*
3. VAT is charged on the subtotal.
4. Calculate total.
5. Copy all formulas using fill down.
6. Format all money amounts to currency.
7. Format headings to bold, as shown.
8. Centre the data in columns B to G.
9. Print the spreadsheet.
10. Save the spreadsheet as **Car Rentals**.

 Spreadsheet Formulas Assignment Nine

Create a new spreadsheet workbook and enter data as shown in Table 1.13. Enter formulas in the shaded cells to complete the spreadsheet.

Table 1.13

	A	B	C	D	E
1	**Product**	**Current Price**	**Increase**	**Projected Price**	**% Increase**
2	Clock calculator	24.34	1.5		
3	Handheld calculator	14.59	0.95		
4	Thesaurus	84.29	5.5		
5	Desktop calculator	45.35	4		
6	Printing calculator	127.95	6.75		
7	Ink roller	37	1.2		
8	Scientific calculator	84.34	3.5		
9	Compact camera	112.73	5		
10	Superzoom camera	204.46	10		

1. The projected price is calculated by adding the increase to the current price.
2. The percentage increase is calculated by dividing the increase by the current price.
3. Copy formulas using fill down.
4. Format cells E2 to E10 to percentage, one decimal place.
5. Format all money amounts to currency.
6. Centre the data in columns B to E.
7. Format headings to bold, as shown.
8. Adjust column widths where necessary.
9. Print the spreadsheet.
10. Save the spreadsheet as **Discount**.

 Spreadsheet Formulas Assignment Ten

Create a new spreadsheet workbook and enter data as shown in Table 1.14 on page 22. Enter formulas in the shaded cells to complete the spreadsheet.

Tip: You can reduce the amount of typing required to set up this spreadsheet by copying the side headings using the copy and paste buttons.

1. Format all interest rates and DIRT tax rates to percentage, one decimal place.
2. Use a formula to read the contents of B1 as principal year 1 for each of the three accounts.
3. The interest is calculated by multiplying the principal by the interest rate.
4. DIRT tax is calculated by multiplying the interest by the DIRT tax rate. (*Hint: use absolute cell references when referring to cells containing interest rates.*)

Table 1.14

	A	B	C	D	E	F
1	Principal	6000				
2						
3	Account 1		Account 2		Account 3	
4	Interest rate:	0.06	Interest rate:	0.069	Interest rate:	0.065
5	DIRT tax:	0.01	DIRT tax:	0.055	DIRT tax:	0.016
6						
7		Account 1	Account 2	Account 3		
8	Principal year 1					
9	Year 1 interest					
10	Year 1 DIRT tax					
11	Adjusted interest					
12	Principal year 2					
13	Year 2 interest					
14	Year 2 DIRT tax					
15	Adjusted interest					
16	Principal year 3					
17	Year 3 interest					
18	Year 3 DIRT tax					
19	Adjusted interest					
20	Principal year 4					
21	Year 4 interest					
22	Year 4 DIRT tax					
23	Adjusted interest					
24	Principal year 5					
25	Year 5 interest					
26	Year 5 DIRT tax					
27	Adjusted interest					
28	Five Year Total					

5. Subtract the DIRT tax from the interest to calculate the adjusted interest.

6. Principal year 2 is calculated by adding the adjusted interest to principal year 1.

7. Use the copy and paste functions to copy the interest, DIRT tax, adjusted interest and principal from year 1 to year 2.

8. Continue using the Paste button to copy the calculations to year 3, year 4 and year 5.

 Note: You only need to click the Copy button once.

9. Print preview the spreadsheet. Click the Setup button and display the gridlines and the row and column headings.

10. Format all money amounts to currency.

11. Format headings to bold, as shown.

12. Centre and align data to the right, as shown.

Figure 1.37

13. Check spellings using the Spelling button.

Figure 1.38

14. Print the spreadsheet.

15. Which account provides the best return on investment?

16. What is the five-year total on accounts 1, 2 and 3 for each of the following investment amounts: €10,000, €20,000, €50,000 and, €100,000?

17. Save the spreadsheet as **Interest Forecaster**.

 Tip: If Excel displays a blue dot in a cell where you've entered a formula, it indicates that there's a circular reference in the formula. A circular reference is where a formula refers to itself, as shown in Table 1.15. The formula to calculate the interest is incorrect because it refers to B3 instead of B2. The formula is referring to itself because the formula is stored in B3. Excel will display a blue dot in B3 to indicate a circular reference.

Table 1.15

	A	B
1	Interest Rate	5%
2	Amount	€2000
3	Interest	=B3*B1

Toolbar Buttons Introduced in Chapter One

Figure 1.39   The **Undo** button

Click this button to undo your last action or command.

Figure 1.40   The **Fill Down** and **Fill Right** mouse pointer shape

When the mouse pointer is this shape, holding down the left mouse button and dragging down or to the right copies the contents of the current cell to cells in the range highlighted. This method is frequently used to copy formulas.

Figure 1.41   The **Adjust Column Width** mouse pointer shape

When the mouse pointer is this shape, dragging to the left will reduce the width of a column or selected columns. Dragging to the right will increase the width of a column or selected columns.

Figure 1.42   The **Center** button

Click this button to centre data in the current cell or range of cells.

Figure 1.43   The **Bold** button

Click this button to display the contents of a cell or range of cells in heavy print.

Figure 1.44   The **Save** button

Click this button to save the current spreadsheet workbook.

Figure 1.45 The **Cut** button

Click this button followed by the Paste button to move data from the current cell or range of cells to another cell or range of cells.

Figure 1.46 The **Paste** button

Click this button to copy the contents of the Clipboard to the current cell or range of cells.

Figure 1.47 The **Copy** button

Click this button followed by the Paste button to copy data from the current cell or range of cells to another cell or range of cells.

Figure 1.48 The **New** button

Click this button to create a new spreadsheet workbook.

Figure 1.49 The **Currency** button

Click this button to apply the currency format to a number in the current cell or to numbers in a range of cells.

Figure 1.50 The **Decrease Decimal** button

Each time you click this button the number of decimal places displayed in the current cell or range of cells decreases by one. If the value in the cell has more decimal places than are displayed, rounding will occur.

Figure 1.51   The **Increase Decimal** button

Each time you click this button the number of decimal places displayed in the current cell or range of cells increases by one. If the value in the cell has more decimal places than are displayed, rounding will occur.

Figure 1.52   The **Percent Style** button

Click this button to apply the Percent Style to a number in the current cell or to numbers in a range of cells. Numbers are multiplied by 100 and displayed with a % sign. For example, 0.5 becomes 50% when the Percent Style button is clicked.

Figure 1.53   The **Print Preview** button

Click this button to get a preview of what the current worksheet or highlighted range will look like on a printed page.

Figure 1.54   The **Print** button

Click this button to print the current worksheet or highlighted range.

Figure 1.55   The **Spelling** button

Click this button to check spellings in the current worksheet or highlighted range.

Figure 1.56   The **Align Right** button

Click this button to align data to the right in the current cell or range of cells.

Review

Create a new spreadsheet workbook and enter data as shown in Table 1.16.

Table 1.16

	A	B	C	D
1	1		Formula 1	=A9–A2*A3+A4/A2
2	2		Formula 2	
3	3		Formula 3	
4	4		Formula 4	
5	5		Formula 5	
6	6		Formula 6	
7	7		Formula 7	
8	8		Formula 8	
9	9		Formula 9	
10	10		Formula 10	

Save this spreadsheet as **Formulas Review**.

Ten formulas are listed in Table 1.17. In each case, first work out the answer to the formula using pen and paper and then check your answer by entering the formula using cell references in the Formulas Review spreadsheet.

Table 1.17

		Write the answer to each formula below
Formula 1	9–2*3+4/2	
Formula 2	1+2*3–8/2	
Formula 3	8–2*3–8/2	
Formula 4	6+2*3–4/2	
Formula 5	(5–3)*(1+4)/4	
Formula 6	(8–6/2+4*5)–((8–6)/2+4*5)	
Formula 7	3+9/3+9/3	
Formula 8	9–4*2–6/2	
Formula 9	6–4/2–6/2	
Formula 10	(9+1+5)/3	

Once you've worked out the answer to a formula, enter the formula, using cell references, in the Formulas Review spreadsheet. Enter your first formula in D1, as shown in Table 1.16, your second formula in D2, your third formula in D3 and so on.

Worked Example

9–2*3+4/2
In any formula that doesn't contain brackets, multiplication and division are always done first.

Step One

2*3=6;4/2=2.

Step Two

The results of any multiplication and division operations will then replace those calculations in the original formula.

- 6 replaces 2*3
- 2 replaces 4/2
- which results in the following formula
- 9–6+2
- giving 5 as the answer.

Now check your answer by entering the formula in cell D1 in the spreadsheet. When we change the numbers to cell references, we get the following spreadsheet formula: =A9–A2*A3+A4/A2.

If your calculations are correct the spreadsheet will give the same answer. Complete formulas two to ten in the same way.

2

Spreadsheet Functions

In Chapter 2, you will learn how to

- Assign a name to a single cell
- Assign a name to a range of cells
- Use the SUM, AVERAGE, MAX, MIN, COUNT and COUNTA functions
- Use advanced functions: POWER, SQRT, DB, SUMIF and COUNTIF.

Spreadsheet Ranges

A spreadsheet range can be defined as two or more cells in a spreadsheet that can be highlighted using any one of the following methods.

1. Clicking and dragging with the mouse.
2. Holding down the Shift key and pressing an arrow key (usually either the down or the right arrow key).
3. Pressing F8 followed by an arrow key.

Ranges are described by referring to the first and the last cell in the range. There are four types of spreadsheet ranges, as shown below.

1. Horizontal range. The range displayed in Figure 2.1 is referred to as A1:C1.

	A	B	C	D
1				
2				

Figure 2.1

2. Vertical range. The range displayed in Figure 2.2 is referred to as A1:A4.

	A	B
1		
2		
3		
4		
5		

Figure 2.2

3. Ranges consisting of two or more rows and columns of cells. The range displayed in Figure 2.3 is referred to as A1:B5.

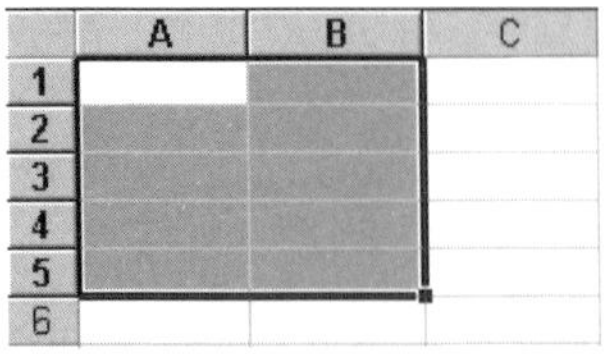

Figure 2.3

 Note: When a single range is highlighted, the first cell in the range is white. All the other cells in the range are shaded.

4. Ranges consisting of cells or groups of cells that are not next to each other. The range displayed in Figure 2.4 is referred to as A1:A5, C1:C5. To highlight multiple ranges hold down the CTRL key when highlighting the second and subsequent ranges.

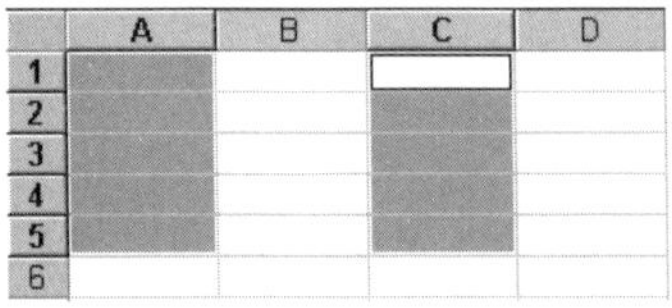

Figure 2.4

Spreadsheet ranges are very important because, as we'll see in the next section, they are used in spreadsheet functions.

Note: When multiple ranges are highlighted, the first cell in the last range that was highlighted is white. All the other cells in the range are shaded.

Spreadsheet Functions

In Chapter 1 we used spreadsheet formulas to do all our calculations. Some of these formulas were quite long and some formulas required correct positioning of brackets. In theory, nearly every spreadsheet calculation could be carried out using a formula. More complicated calculations may require a number of formulas. Fortunately, the people who developed spreadsheets realised that the need to use complex formulas in a spreadsheet would have two major implications.

1. Spreadsheet users would have to spend a lot of time developing formulas.
2. The more complex the formula, the greater the chance of an error being made.

Spreadsheet functions were developed for these reasons. Each function is programmed to carry out a specific task such as adding, calculating averages, finding the highest number in a list or calculating depreciation of an asset. Simply refer to the function by name and it does all the calculation work for you. In cases where a calculation can be performed using either a function or a formula, both methods will give the same result but the function method is usually quicker and requires less effort. Less mental effort is needed because the spreadsheet does the calculations for you. Less time and physical effort is required because you won't need to type as much. Some of the more popular functions are listed below in Table 2.1.

Table 2.1

Function name	Action	Example (Single range)	Example (Multiple ranges)
SUM	Adds numbers in a range of cells or multiple ranges	=sum(B4:B15)	=sum(B4:B15,E4:E15)
AVERAGE	Calculates the average of numbers in a range of cells or multiple ranges	=average(B4:B15)	=average(B4:B15, E4:E15)
MAX	Finds the highest number in a range of cells or multiple ranges	=max(B4:B15)	=max(B4:B15,E4:E15)
MIN	Finds the lowest number in a range of cells or multiple ranges	=min(B4:B15)	=min(B4:B15,E4:E15)
COUNT	Counts the number of cells that contain numbers in a range of cells or multiple ranges	=count(B4:B15)	=count(C4:C15,F4:F15)
COUNTA	Counts the number of cells that are not empty in a range of cells or multiple ranges	=counta(A4:A15)	=counta(D4:D15, G4:G15)

It's worth noting that these functions represent only a small percentage of the full list of functions available in Excel. Specialist functions are available for maths and trigonometry, statistical and financial analysis as well as engineering applications.

Even spreadsheet experts don't know *all* the functions. The functions you will learn and use depends on the type of calculations you're doing with the spreadsheet. The functions listed above are common to nearly every application.

Syntax of a Spreadsheet Function

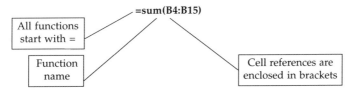

=sum(B4:B15)

All functions start with =

Function name

Cell references are enclosed in brackets

All spreadsheet functions have a similar structure or syntax. A function starts with = and must include a name, such as SUM or AVERAGE. The function name is usually followed by two cell references separated by a colon and these cell references are enclosed in brackets.

Functions vs. Formulas

In the following example we will see how some calculations can be performed using a function or a formula. We will also see that sometimes only a function can be used for a particular calculation.

Table 2.2

	A	B	C	D
1	Business Travel Analysis			
2			2002	
3		Distance Travelled	Business Trips Abroad	Outside EU?
4	January	1244		
5	February	1450	1	Yes
6	March	1155		
7	April	1632	2	
8	May	1871		
9	June	2193	3	
10	July	2500	2	
11	August	3410		
12	September	3685		
13	October	2177	1	Yes
14	November	2450	2	
15	December	1804	4	
16				
17		2002		
18	Total Distance Travelled			
19	Average Mileage per Month			

(Contd.)

Table 2.2 *(Contd.)*

	A	B	C	D
20	Highest Monthly Mileage			
21	Lowest Monthly Mileage			
22	Months with Foreign Travel			
23	Trips Outside EU			

Calculating Total Distance Travelled

Method 1: Formula

$$=B4+B5+B6+B7+B8+B9+B10+B11+B12+B13+B14+B15$$

This gives **25571** as the total distance travelled. In an addition formula, we must refer to every cell that we're adding; the more cells that we're adding, the longer the formula becomes. Long formulas cause two problems. First, they take longer to write and second, the longer a formula, the greater the chance you'll make a mistake when writing it.

Method 2: The SUM Function

$$=sum(B4:B15)$$

This gives **25571** as the total distance travelled. In the SUM function, instead of referring to every cell that we're adding, we simply refer to the range of cells that contains the numbers we're adding. As you can see, the function is much shorter than the formula and will give the same answer.

Calculating Average Distance Travelled per Month

Method 1: Formula

$$=(B4+B5+B6+B7+B8+B9+B10+B11+B12+B13+B14+B15)/12$$

This gives **2130.9** as the average mileage per month. To get the average, we must first add all the numbers together and then divide by the number of months. Brackets are required so that the addition is carried out before the division.

Method 2: The AVERAGE Function

$$=average(B4:B15)$$

This gives **2130.9** as the average distance travelled per month. The AVERAGE function adds all numbers contained in a range of cells and then divides by the number of numbers contained in that range of cells. In this case the AVERAGE function adds all numbers contained in B4 to B15 inclusive and then divides by twelve.

Finding the Highest Monthly Distance Travelled and the Lowest Monthly Distance Travelled

If we look at the distances travelled for each of the twelve months we can see that September was the month with the highest mileage and March has the lowest mileage. It isn't possible to figure this out using a formula so we must rely entirely on functions to find the highest and lowest monthly distance travelled.

Method 1: The MAX Function

=max(B4:B15)

This gives **3685** as the highest monthly distance travelled. The MAX function finds the highest number in a range of cells. In this case the MAX function looks at cells B4 to B15 inclusive and displays 3685 as the highest number in that range of cells.

Method 2: The MIN Function

=min(B4:B15)

This gives **1155** as the lowest monthly distance travelled. The MIN function finds the lowest number in a range of cells. In this case the MIN function looks at cells B4 to B15 inclusive and displays 1155 as the lowest number in that range of cells.

 Note: Without the MAX and MIN functions, finding the highest and lowest number in a group of numbers would require a computer program.

Counting the Number of Months with Foreign Travel

It's relatively easy to count numbers in a list when you can see all the numbers on one screen. In longer lists, there's a greater chance of making a mistake when counting. This is where the COUNT function is particularly useful.

 Note: Again, there's no formula for this calculation. A computer program would be required.

The COUNT Function

=count(C4:C15)

This gives **7** as the number of months with foreign travel. The COUNT function counts the number of cells that contain numbers in a range of cells. In this case the COUNT function looks at cells C4 to C15 inclusive and displays 7 as the number of cells containing numbers in that range. It's important to note that the COUNT function will also count zeros. If we had entered zero as the number of business trips abroad for January, March, May, August and September, the

COUNT function would have calculated twelve as the number of months with foreign travel.

Counting the Number of Trips Outside the EU

The COUNTA Function

=counta(D4:D15)

This gives **2** as the number of trips outside the EU. The COUNTA function counts the number of cells that aren't empty in a range of cells. In this case the COUNTA function looks at cells D4 to D15 inclusive and displays 2 as the number of cells in that range that aren't empty. Since the COUNT function only counts numeric cell entries, the COUNTA function is useful if we need to count text cell entries or a mixture of text and numeric cell entries.

Using Functions with Multiple Ranges

Continuing the example, travel figures for 2003 have been entered in Table 2.3 on page 36. Totals for 2003 have been calculated using the SUM, AVERAGE, MAX, MIN, COUNT and COUNTA functions.

We will use functions with multiple ranges to carry out the two-year analysis. When referring to more than one range in a function, ranges must be separated with commas.

Example

=sum(B4:B15, E4:E15)

This function calculates the total distance travelled over two years by adding numbers in column B and column E.

Calculating Total Distance Travelled Over Two Years

=sum(B4:B15, E4:E15)

This gives **51905** as the total distance travelled. This could also be calculated using the formula =B18+C18 or by using the function/formula combination

=sum(B4:B15) + sum(E4:E15)

Calculating Average Distance Travelled per Month Over Two Years

=average(B4:B15, E4:E15)

This gives **2162.7** as the average distance travelled per month. This could also have been calculated using the formula =(B19+C19)/2, which adds the 2002 average to the 2003 average and then divides by two, or by using the formula =D18/24, which divides the total traveled over two years by 24 months.

Table 2.3

	A	B	C	D	E	F	G
1	Business Travel Analysis						
2		2002			2003		
3		Distance Travelled	Business Trips Abroad	Outside EU?	Distance Travelled	Business Trips Abroad	Outside EU?
4	January	1244			1066	2	
5	February	1450	1	Yes	1522	1	Yes
6	March	1155			1716		
7	April	1632	2		1088	2	
8	May	1871			2044		
9	June	2193	3		1989	2	
10	July	2500	2		2750	2	
11	August	3410			3400	1	Yes
12	September	3685			3890	2	
13	October	2177	1	Yes	2544	1	Yes
14	November	2450	2		2525	2	
15	December	1804	4		1800	2	
16							
17		2002	2003		2 Year Analysis		
18	Total Distance Travelled	25571	26334	=sum(B4:B15,E4:E15)=51905			
19	Average Mileage per Month	2130.9	2194.5	=average(B4:B15,E4:E15) =2162.7			
20	Highest Monthly Mileage	3685	3890	=max(B4:B15,E4:E15) =3890			
21	Lowest Monthly Mileage	1155	1066	=min(B4: B15,E4:E15) =1066			
22	Months with Foreign Travel	7	10	=count(C4:C15,F4:F15)=17			
23	Trips Outside EU	2	3	=counta(D4:D15,G4:G15)=5			

Each function does calculations based on 2 ranges of numbers, which are highlighted above

Finding the Highest Monthly Distance Travelled and the Lowest Monthly Distance Travelled Over Two Years

=max(B4:B15,E4:E15)

This gives **3890** as the highest monthly distance travelled. This could also have been calculated using =max(B20:C20) which would find the higher of 3685 and 3890.

=min(B4:B15,E4:E15)

This gives **1066** as the lowest monthly distance travelled. This could also have been calculated using =min(B21:C21) which would find the lower of 1155 and 1066.

Counting the Number of Months with Foreign Travel Over Two Years

=count(C4:C15,F4:F15)

This gives **17** as the number of months with foreign travel. This could also have been calculated using the formula =B22+C22.

Counting the Number of Trips Outside the EU Over Two Years

=counta(D4:D15,G4:G15)

This gives **5** as the number of trips outside the EU. This could also have been calculated using the formula =B23+C23.

It can be seen from the above example that many calculations can be performed using either a formula, a function or a combination of both. It's good spreadsheet practice to use a mixture of formulas and functions in your calculations.

Recommendations for Using Spreadsheet Functions

1. Use of the arithmetic operators (*/+–) inside the brackets of a SUM or AVERAGE function can lead to errors.

Example: Correct Use of the SUM Function

=sum(B4:B15)

This adds all the numbers in the range B4:B15, giving 25571.

Example: Incorrect Use of the SUM Function

> Using + – * / inside the brackets of a function can lead to errors

=sum(B4+B15)

This only adds the first and last number in the range B4:B15, giving 3048.

2. The SUM function should only be used for addition. Formulas should be used for subtraction, multiplication and division.

3. A function will always have brackets, but not all formulas have brackets.

Spreadsheet Functions Assignment One

Create a new spreadsheet workbook and enter data as shown in Table 2.4. Enter functions in the shaded cells to complete the spreadsheet.

Tip: The match names can be copied using the fill handle.

Table 2.4

	A	B	C	D	E	F	G	H
1	United Football Club							
2		Attempts on Goal	Wides	Fouls	Goals Scored	Goals Conceded	Corners	Free Kicks
3	Match 1	5	4	15	1	2	2	5
4	Match 2	7	3	20	2	1	1	6
5	Match 3	6	6	22	0	0	4	3
6	Match 4	10	5	11	2	1	3	5
7	Match 5	4	2	17	2	3	5	4
8	Match 6	5	4	9	1	2	0	2
9	Match 7	9	3	18	3	2	1	8
10	Match 8	6	2	14	0	1	3	7
11	Match 9	5	3	10	1	2	1	6
12	Match 10	8	5	17	2	3	2	10
13								
14	Total							
15	Average							
16	Highest							
17	Lowest							

1. Wrap text within cells in row 2, as shown, using Format, Cells, Alignment and Wrap Text.

Format Painter button

Figure 2.5

 Tip: With the cell pointer in a cell where the text has been wrapped, click the Format Painter button and then highlight other cells where you want to wrap the text.

2. Calculate total attempts on goal using the SUM function.
3. Calculate average attempts on goal using the AVERAGE function.
4. Calculate highest attempts on goal using the MAX function.
5. Calculate lowest attempts on goal using the MIN function.
6. Copy all functions using fill right.

 Tip: Highlight B14:B17 first. Next, copy all functions using the fill handle. Remember, it's a white cross for highlighting and a black cross for copying.

7. Format headings to bold, as shown.
8. Centre the data in columns B to H.
9. Save the spreadsheet as **United Football Club**.

 Spreadsheet Functions Example Two

In Table 2.5 we can see how a function works with ranges consisting of two or more rows and columns of cells.

Table 2.5

	A	B	C	D	E
1	**Rainfall (mm) Analysis**				
2		Roches Point	Valentia	Loop Head	Erris Head
3	Monday	0	5	3	2.5
4	Tuesday	10	12	11	8
5	Wednesday	0	0	0	0
6	Thursday	5	8	7	6
7	Friday	0	0	0	0
8	Saturday	0	0	0	5
9	Sunday	14	12	10	6

(Contd.)

Table 2.5 *(Contd.)*

	A	B	C	D	E
10			Each function does calculations on the range B3:E9 which is		
11	South/West Weekly Rainfall Summary		highlighted on the previous page.		
12	Total (mm)		=sum(B3:E9) gives 124.5		
13	Average (mm)		=average(B3:E9) gives 4.4		
14	Highest Daily Amount (mm)		=max(B3:E9) gives 14		
15	Lowest Daily Amount (mm)		=min(B3:E9) gives 0		

 Spreadsheet Functions Assignment Two

Create a new spreadsheet workbook and enter data as shown in Table 2.6. Enter functions in the shaded cells to complete the spreadsheet.

Table 2.6

	A	B	C	D	E	F	G
1	Western Area Sales					Date	
2							
3		JAN	FEB	MAR	APR	MAY	JUN
4	Unit 1	2076	2971	2241	2503	2418	2063
5	Unit 2	3510	2085	3394	2957	2048	2279
6	Unit 3	1866	1600	1750	1780	1800	1975
7	Unit 4	1200	1341	1200	1453	1098	1255
8	Unit 5	1209	2089	2500	2368	2044	2100
9	Unit 6	1531	2311	1855	1762	1455	1500
10	Unit 7	2087	1993	2000	2450	2369	2100
11							
12	Monthly Unit Sales Analysis						
13	Total Sales						
14	Average Sales						
15	Highest Sales Achieved						

(Contd.)

Table **2.6** (*Contd.*)

	A	B	C	D	E	F	G
16	**Lowest Sales Achieved**						
17							
18				**Western Area Six Month Totals**			
19				**Total Western Area Sales**			
20				**Average Western Area Sales**			
21				**Six-Month Sales High**			
22				**Six-Month Sales Low**			

1. Enter today's date in G1 (*typing =today() inserts the date from the computer clock*).
2. Calculate total sales, average sales, highest sales achieved and lowest sales achieved for each month. Copy these functions using fill right.
3. Calculate total western area sales, average western area sales, six-month sales high and six-month sales low (*these calculations are based on sales figures for units one to seven over six months*).
4. Format all averages to zero decimal places.
5. Format headings to bold, as shown.
6. Centre the data, as shown.
7. Save the spreadsheet as **Western Sales Analysis**.

When Should You Use a Function?

Usually we can get the answer with a function quicker than if we used a formula, but this doesn't mean that we should always use functions. An experienced spreadsheet user will use a combination of formulas and functions as the need arises. New spreadsheet users often forget about formulas once they learn how to create functions. It's good spreadsheet practice to use a combination of formulas and functions. As a general rule, if a formula is long and complicated consider using a function. Most basic calculations can be performed using formulas. Sometimes it will be more appropriate to use a formula, as outlined below.

Table **2.7**

	A	B	C	D	E	F	G	H	I
1	Artist	Date	Stalls	%Full	Circle	%Full	Balcony	%Full	Total Tickets
2	The Corrs	08/09/03	150	50%	300	85.7%	220	88%	

To calculate the total tickets for The Corrs, we must add 150, 300 and 220. In this case we must use the formula =C2+E2+G2, giving 670 as the total tickets. Using the SUM function =sum(C2:G2) would add the percentages as well as the ticket sales, incorrectly giving 671.357 as the total tickets.

Tip: When creating functions, rather than typing the cell range, type the function name followed by an open bracket and then highlight the range of cells. When you do this, Excel types the cell range for you. For example, to add numbers in the range A2:A10, firstly type =sum followed by an open bracket. Next, highlight from A2 to A10 and close the bracket. Creating functions using this method reduces the chances of making a mistake.

Spreadsheet Functions Assignment Three

Create a new spreadsheet workbook and enter data as shown in Table 2.8 on page 43. Use a combination of formulas and functions to complete the spreadsheet.

Tip: A date can be entered in shortened form, e.g. type 8/9/3 and press Enter. The date will be displayed as 08/09/2003 or 08/09/03 depending on how your spreadsheet is set up.

1. Insert the date using the Today function (*typing =today() inserts the date from the computer clock*).
2. Calculate the total sales, average sales, highest sales, lowest sales and number of performances in the stalls. Use Copy and Paste to copy the functions that calculate the total, average, highest and lowest sales to the circle and the balcony.

Note: In this case, the fill handle can't be used to copy the functions because this would also copy functions to columns D and E where they are not required.

3. Calculate the percentage of the stalls that was full, the percentage of the circle that was full, and the percentage of the balcony that was full for each performance. Format these cells using the Percent Style button.
4. Calculate the total tickets sold for each performance.
5. Calculate the percentage of the venue that was full for each performance. Format these cells using the Percent Style button.
6. Print the spreadsheet with gridlines and row and column headings displayed.
7. Save the spreadsheet as **Rock Café**.

Advanced Functions

The POWER Function

The POWER function calculates the result of a number raised to a power (where you multiply a number by itself a number of times). For example, 2×2 is 2^2 or 2

Table 2.8

	A	B	C	D	E	F	G	H	I	J
1	Rock Café								Date	
2										
3								Stalls	300	
4								Circle	350	
5								Balcony	250	
6										
7	Artist	Date	Stalls	%Full	Circle	%Full	Balcony	%Full	Total Tickets	%Full
8	The Corrs	08/09/03	150		300		220			
9	The Frames	10/09/03	276		245		141			
10	Aslan	11/09/03	290		307		209			
11	Jack L	14/09/03	250		312		196			
12	Westlife	18/09/03	300		350		250			
13	Ronan Keating	19/09/03	100		267		233			
14	Brian Kennedy	20/09/03	180		255		200			
15										
16	Total Sales									
17	Average Sales									
18	Highest Sales									
19	Lowest Sales									
20	Number of Performances									

to the power of 2; $2 \times 2 \times 2$ is 2^3 or 2 to the power of 3; $2 \times 2 \times 2 \times 2$ is 2^4 or 2 to the power of 4, and so on. A common use of this would be where we're calculating the area of a circle. To calculate the area of a circle, we must square the radius and multiply the result by pi (3.14). In Table 2.9 on page 44 a circle radius of five has been entered in A2, the square of the circle radius is calculated using =power(A2, 2). The square is multiplied by 3.14 giving 78.5 as the circle radius.

Another application of the POWER function is in the conversion of kilobytes, megabytes and gigabytes into bytes. A kilobyte is equal to 2^{10} bytes. A megabyte is equal to 2^{20} bytes. A gigabyte is equal to 2^{30} bytes.

Example One: Calculating the Area of a Circle Using the POWER Function

Table 2.9

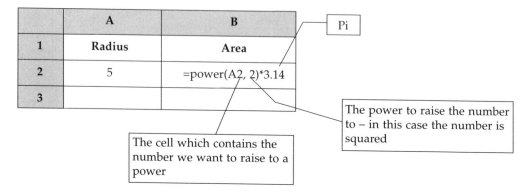

	A	B
1	Radius	Area
2	5	=power(A2, 2)*3.14
3		

Pi

The cell which contains the number we want to raise to a power

The power to raise the number to – in this case the number is squared

Example Two: Calculating the Number of Bytes Using the POWER Function

Table 2.10

	A	B	C	D
1				
2	1	kilobyte equals	= power(2,10)*A2	Bytes
3	1	megabyte equals	= power(2,20)*A3	Bytes
4	1	gigabyte equals	= power(2,30)*A4	Bytes

 Spreadsheet Functions Assignment Four

Create a new spreadsheet workbook and enter data as shown in Table 2.11. Enter functions in the shaded cells to complete the spreadsheet.

Table 2.11

	A	B	C
1	Circle Radius (cm)	Area	
2	25		
3	15		
4	31		
5	59		
6	12		

1. Calculate the area of each circle using the POWER function.
2. Format headings to bold and centre the data, as shown.
3. Save the spreadsheet as **Circle Area Calculator**.

 Spreadsheet Functions Assignment Five

Create a new spreadsheet workbook and enter data as shown in Table 2.12. Enter functions in the shaded cells to complete the spreadsheet.

Table 2.12

	A	B	C	D
1	Byte Converter			
2				
3	512	Kilobyte Cache =		Bytes
4	256	Megabytes of RAM =		Bytes
5	16	Megabytes Video Memory =		Bytes
6	40	Gigabyte Hard Disk =		Bytes

1. Enter functions in the shaded cells to complete the spreadsheet. (*Multiply by* 2^{10} *to convert from kilobytes to bytes, by* 2^{20} *to convert from megabytes to bytes and by* 2^{30} *to convert from gigabytes to bytes.*)
2. Format data as shown above.
3. Save the spreadsheet as **Byte Converter**.

 Tip: If you want to use a number in a formula or function, always enter that number in a separate cell. Table 2.13 is correct because the number and the text were entered in separate cells.

Table 2.13

	A	B
3	512	Kilobyte Cache =

Table 2.14 on page 46 is incorrect because the number and the text were entered in the same cell. We would be unable to use 512 in a calculation because the spreadsheet interprets A3 as text and not as a number. The #VALUE error message will be displayed if A3 is referred to in a formula or function.

Table 2.14

	A
3	512 **Kilobyte Cache** =

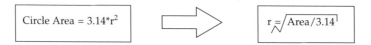

The SQRT Function

The SQRT function calculates the square root of a number. A common use of this would be where we know the area of a circle and we want to calculate the radius

| Circle Area = $3.14*r^2$ | $\Rightarrow$ | $r = \sqrt{Area/3.14}$ |

From the above it can be seen that the radius of a circle is calculated by getting the square root of the area divided by 3.14.

In the example below, a circle area of 78.5 has been entered in A2. The radius of the circle is calculated using =sqrt(A2/3.14), which gives five as the radius.

Example Three: Calculating the Radius of a Circle Using the SQRT Function

Table 2.15

	A	B
1	**Circle Area**	**Radius**
2	78.5	=sqrt(A2/3.14) → Pi
3		

Area of the circle

Spreadsheet Functions Assignment Six

Create a new spreadsheet workbook and enter data as shown in Table 2.16 on page 47. Enter functions in the shaded cells to complete the spreadsheet.

1. Enter functions in the shaded cells to complete the spreadsheet.
2. Format data as shown.
3. Save the spreadsheet as **Circle Radius Calculator**.

The DB Function (Declining Balance)

The DB function calculates the depreciation of an asset over a number of years, using the declining balance method. The DB function requires

Table 2.16

	A	B	C
1	Circle Radius Calculator		
2			
3	Circle Area	Radius	
4	314		
5	1256		
6	2826		
7	5024		
8	7850		

four items of information, known as arguments, in order to calculate depreciation. These are as follows.

- Purchase price or initial value of the asset
- Disposal value of the asset after the depreciation period
- Number of years over which to depreciate the asset
- Year number.

Example Four: Calculating Annual Depreciation Using the DB Function

Table 2.17

	A	B	C	D	E
1	Asset:	Company Van		Purchase Price:	€20000
2				Disposal Value:	€5000
3				Expected Life (years):	5
4					
5	Year 1 depreciation	=DB($E$1,$E$2,$E$3,1) gives €4840			
6	Year 2 depreciation	=DB($E$1,$E$2,$E$3,2) gives €3668.72			
7	Year 3 depreciation	=DB($E$1,$E$2,$E$3,3) gives €2780.89			
8	Year 4 depreciation	=DB($E$1,$E$2,$E$3,4) gives €2107.91			
9	Year 5 depreciation	=DB($E$1,$E$2,$E$3,5) gives €1597.80			

Purchase Price (€20000) | Disposal Value (€5000) | Number of years over which the asset is depreciated (5) | Year Number

Spreadsheet Functions Assignment Seven

Create a new spreadsheet workbook and enter data as shown. Enter functions in the shaded cells to complete the spreadsheet.

Table 2.18

	A	B	C	D	E
1	Depreciation Schedule				
2					
3	Asset	Company Car	Machinery	Computer	Truck
4	Purchase Price	24500	120000	2300	42800
5	Disposal Value	8500	20000	300	12500
6	Expected Life(years)	5	8	4	6
7					
8	Year 1 depreciation				
9	Year 2 depreciation				
10	Year 3 depreciation				
11	Year 4 depreciation				
12	Year 5 depreciation				
13	Year 6 depreciation				
14	Year 7 depreciation				
15	Year 8 depreciation				

1. Enter functions in the shaded cells to complete the spreadsheet. (**Hint:** *The functions can be copied using fill right.*)
2. Format all money amounts to currency.
3. Format headings to bold and centre data, as shown.
4. Save the spreadsheet as **Depreciation Schedule**.

The SUMIF Function

The SUMIF function adds cell values in a range if they satisfy a given condition. This is very useful if there are values relating to different items in the same row or column and these values are in random order. In the example below sales values relating to apples, bananas and pears have been entered in column C. The SUMIF function can be used to calculate total sales for each of the three products.

Example: Calculating Sales by Product Using the SUMIF Function

Table 2.19

	A	B	C	D	E
1	**Monday Sales**				
2					
3	**Customer**	**Product**	**Amount**		
4	Tony Leahy	Apples	250		
5	Sinead Donovan	Bananas	100		
6	Peter Smith	Apples	300		
7	Stephen Connors	Pears	75		
8	Seamus O Neill	Bananas	80		
9	Gary Jennings	Bananas	150		
10	Mike Healy	Apples	200		
11	Eileen Carr	Pears	300		
12	Christine Flynn	Apples	50		
13					
14	Total Sales of Apples	=sumif(B4:B12,"Apples",C4:C12) *gives 800*			
15	Total Sales of Bananas	=sumif(B4:B12,"Bananas",C4:C12) *gives 330*			
16	Total Sales of Pears	=sumif(B4:B12,"Pears",C4:C12) *gives 375*			

Only add numbers from this range which satisfy the condition, i.e. numbers relating to Pears

Range of cells to be evaluated

Which cells in the range B4:12 contain the word "Pears"

Spreadsheet Functions Assignment Eight

Create a new spreadsheet workbook and enter data as shown in Table 2.20 on page 50. Enter functions in the shaded cells to complete the spreadsheet.

1. Calculate the total hours worked by each mechanic using the SUMIF function.
2. Calculate total pay using a formula.
3. Format all numbers relating to hours worked to one decimal place.
4. Format all money amounts to currency.
5. Format headings to bold and align data as shown.
6. Save the spreadsheet as **Pay Calculator**.

Table 2.20

	A	B	C	D
1	Main Street Car Repairs			
2				
3	Date	Description	Mechanic	Hours
4	02/06/03	Standard Service	Pat	1.5
5	02/06/03	Clutch	Dave	4
6	02/06/03	Gearbox	Pat	6
7	02/06/03	Standard Service	Dave	2
8	02/06/03	Puncture	Dave	0.2
9	02/06/03	Clutch	Pat	3
10	02/06/03	Timing Belt	Dave	5.5
11	03/06/03	Puncture	Pat	0.1
12	03/06/03	Standard Service	Pat	2
13	03/06/03	Puncture	Pat	0.2
14	03/06/03	Puncture	Pat	0.2
15	03/06/03	Clutch	Dave	3
16	03/06/03	Gearbox	Dave	6
17	03/06/03	Timing Belt	Pat	4
18				
19	Mechanic	Total Hours	Hourly Rate	Total Pay
20	Pat		25.5	
21	Dave		25.5	

 The COUNTIF Function

The COUNTIF function counts the number of cells in a range that satisfy a given condition.

Example: Analysis of Jobs by Department and Month Using the COUNTIF Function

=countif(C4:C11, A16)

Table 2.21

	A	B	C	D
1	Maintenance Department Work Log			
2				
3	Month	Work Done	Department	
4	June	Painting	Finance	
5	June	Cleaning	Sales	
6	July	Install new PCs	Computer	
7	July	Service alarm	Sales	
8	July	Painting	Finance	
9	July	Service alarm	Finance	
10	August	Cleaning	Sales	
11	August	Painting	Computer	
12				
13	Analysis of Jobs by Department		Monthly Job Count	
14	Finance	=COUNTIF(C4:C11,A14) *gives 3*	June	=COUNTIF(A4:A11,C14) *gives 2*
15	Sales	=COUNTIF(C4:C11,A15) *gives 3*	July	=COUNTIF(A4:A11,C15) *gives 4*
16	Computer	=COUNTIF(C4:C11,A16) *gives 2*	August	=COUNTIF(A4:A11,C16) *gives 2*
17				

Range of cells to be evaluated

Range of cells to be evaluated

Count the number of cells in the range C4:C11 which contain the text "Computer" which is stored in A16

Count the number of cells in the range A4:A11 which contain the text "August" which is stored in C16

This COUNTIF function checks to see how many cells in the range C4:C11 match what's stored in A16, i.e. how many cells in the range C4:C11 contain the text 'Computer'. The function will give 2 as the answer.

Spreadsheet Functions Assignment Nine

Create a new spreadsheet workbook and enter data as shown in Table 2.22 on page 52. Enter functions in the shaded cells to complete the spreadsheet.

1. Calculate the number of problems reported by each employee.
2. Calculate the number of times each problem occurred.

Table 2.22

	A	B	C	D	E
1	Tech Support Call Analysis				
2					
3	Referred By	Date	Problem	Total Problems Referred By	
4	John Hall	02/09/03	Hard Disk	John Hall	
5	Evelyn Smith	05/09/03	Operating System	Evelyn Smith	
6	Tom O Donoghue	05/09/03	Printer	Tom O Donoghue	
7	Joan Donovan	05/09/03	Word 2000	Joan Donovan	
8	Joan Donovan	06/09/03	Word 2000	Peter Jones	
9	Tom O Donoghue	06/09/03	Windows XP		
10	Joan Donovan	07/09/03	Word 2000	**Types of Problem**	
11	Evelyn Smith	07/09/03	Excel 2000	Hard Disk	
12	Joan Donovan	07/09/03	Windows XP	Floppy Disk	
13	Peter Jones	07/09/03	Floppy Disk	Operating System	
14	John Hall	07/09/03	Hard Disk	Printer	
15	Tom O Donoghue	08/09/03	Printer	Word 2000	
16	Peter Jones	08/09/03	Windows XP	Excel 2000	
17	Evelyn Smith	08/09/03	Excel 2000	Windows XP	

3. Copy both functions using fill down. (**Hint**: *You'll get incorrect results if you don't use absolute cell references.*)

4. Format the data as shown above.

5. Save the spreadsheet as **Tech Support**.

 Tip: The SUMIF and COUNTIF functions will only give a result if exact matches are found. For example, there were two hard disk problems. If a spelling error was made and 'Hard Dosk' was incorrectly entered in C14, the COUNTIF function will not include this in its count. Unnecessary use of the spacebar also leads to problems here. Hard Disk, typed with no space after the letter 'k', is not the same as Hard Disk typed with a space after the letter 'k'. Remember, SUMIF and COUNTIF must find an exact match.

Spreadsheet Functions Assignment Ten

Create a new spreadsheet workbook and enter data as shown in Table 2.23. Enter functions in the shaded cells to complete the spreadsheet.

 Tip: The exam numbers can be copied using fill series. Enter the first exam number in A4. Next, highlight A4:A23, using the white cross mouse pointer. Select **Edit** followed by **Fill** from the menu. Select **Series** and then click OK.

Table 2.23

	A	B	C	D
1	Exam Analysis			
2				
3	Exam Number	Centre	Marker	Result
4	102511	Castlebar	Brian Williams	Pass
5	102512	Sligo	Sarah Jones	Fail
6	102513	Galway	Brian Williams	Pass
7	102514	Galway	Susan Kinsella	Merit
8	102515	Sligo	Brian Williams	Merit
9	102516	Castlebar	Sarah Jones	Pass
10	102517	Sligo	Brian Williams	Distinction
11	102518	Sligo	Sarah Jones	Fail
12	102519	Galway	Sarah Jones	Distinction
13	102520	Galway	Susan Kinsella	Pass
14	102521	Castlebar	Brian Williams	Pass
15	102522	Galway	Susan Kinsella	Fail
16	102523	Sligo	Brian Williams	Fail
17	102524	Castlebar	Susan Kinsella	Merit
18	102525	Castlebar	Susan Kinsella	Distinction
19	102526	Galway	Brian Williams	Merit
20	102527	Sligo	Sarah Jones	Fail

(Contd.)

Table 2.23 *(Contd.)*

	A	B	C	D
21	102528	Sligo	Susan Kinsella	Merit
22	102529	Sligo	Susan Kinsella	Pass
23	102530	Galway	Brian Williams	Pass
24				
25	**Exam Centre**	**Number of Students Examined**	**Marker**	**Number of Exams Corrected**
26	Castlebar		Brian Williams	
27	Sligo		Sarah Jones	
28	Galway		Susan Kinsella	

1. Calculate the number of students examined in each center.
2. Calculate the number of exams corrected by each examiner.
3. Format the data as shown above.
4. Save the spreadsheet as **Exam Correction Analysis**.

Naming Cells in a Spreadsheet

A name can be assigned to an individual cell or range of cells, thus making formulas easier to understand and remember. It's a good idea to name a cell if that cell is frequently referred to by formulas or functions.

Example: Assigning a Name to a Single Cell

In Table 2.24 on page 55, calculating the discount for each product requires the use of an absolute cell reference. The reference to G2 (the cell containing the discount rate) is absolute so that when the formula =E6*$G$2 is copied to calculate discounts for the remaining products, the reference to G2 doesn't change.

Formulas using absolute references can be quite difficult to write, especially if you have to scroll vertically or horizontally to determine what the absolute cell reference should be. Absolute cell references are also difficult to remember. You may find yourself asking, 'Was that number in A10 or B10?' and then moving to that area of the spreadsheet just to check. This is time consuming and can also lead to errors in formulas. The solution is to name the cell and then refer to that name in the formula instead of using an absolute cell reference.

Table 2.24

	A	B	C	D	E	F	G
1	Building Supplies Invoice						
2						Discount	5%
3							
4							
5	**Product Code**	**Description**	**Quantity**	**Price**	**Total**	**Discount**	
6	200	Sandpaper	20	0.19	= C6*D6	= E6*$G$2	
7	305	Wood Filler	2	6.34	= C7*D7	= E7*$G$2	
8	307	Filling Knife	1	7.22	= C8*D8	= E8*$G$2	
9	451	Pine Cornice	3	8.38	= C9*D9	= E9*$G$2	
10	178	Matt Varnish	1	15.99	= C10*D10	= E10*$G$2	

How to Name a Cell

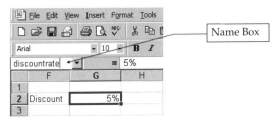

Figure 2.6

1. Select the cell that you want to name.
2. Click in the name box and type the name you want to assign to that cell (spaces are not allowed), then press Enter.

(**Note**: The name will not be accepted unless you press Enter. Clicking the mouse does not work in this case.)

In Table 2.25 on page 56, we have assigned the name discountrate to cell G2. Now we can rewrite our formulas using cell names instead of absolute cell references.

Formulas that refer to cell names are much easier to remember. A cell name is absolute so it will always refer to the same cell no matter where you move or copy it to. Cell names can also be used to refer to cells in other worksheets within the workbook.

Names can also be assigned to spreadsheet ranges. This is useful if you frequently refer to a particular range of cells in calculations and also when there are so many cells in the range that it's too big to fit in the spreadsheet window.

Table 2.25

	Formula (Absolute Ref)	Formula (Cell Name)
Discount (Sandpaper)	=E6*$G$2	=E6*discountrate
Discount (Wood Filler)	=E7*$G$2	=E7*discountrate
Discount (Filling Knife)	=E8*$G$2	=E8*discountrate
Discount (Pine Cornice)	=E9*$G$2	=E9*discountrate
Discount (Matte Varnish)	=E10*$G$2	=E10*discountrate

Example: Assigning a Name to a Range of Cells

In Table 2.26, we need to refer to the range B4:B11 with a number of functions to calculate average, highest and lowest marks as well as number of exams. To make the functions easier to understand and use, we'll assign the name mathsresults

Table 2.26

	A	B
1	Analysis of Exam Results	
2		
3		Maths
4	Tom Boyle	89
5	Mick Gavin	44
6	William Treacy	53
7	Sharon Byrne	70
8	Jaki McKay	66
9	Derek McCormack	30
10	Eileen Nolan	24
11	Margaret O Connell	59
12		
13	Average Mark	
14	Highest Mark	
15	Lowest Mark	
16	Number of Exams	

to the range B4:B11. This is done by highlighting the range, as shown in Figure 2.7, typing mathsresults in the name box and pressing Enter.

mathsresults ▼	= 89
A	**B**
1 Analysis of Exam Results	
2	
3	Maths
4 Tom Boyle	89
5 Mick Gavin	44
6 William Treacy	53
7 Sharon Byrne	70
8 Jaki McKay	66
9 Derek McCormack	30
10 Eileen Nolan	24
11 Margaret O Connell	59
12	
13 Average Mark	
14 Highest Mark	
15 Lowest Mark	
16 Number of Exams	

Figure 2.7

We can now use mathsresults instead of B4:B11 in all functions.

Table 2.27

	Function (Cell Refs)	Function (Range Name)
Average Mark	=average(B4:B11)	=average(mathsresults)
Highest Mark	=max(B4:B11)	=max(mathsresults)
Lowest Mark	=min(B4:B11)	=min(mathsresults)
Number of Exams	=count(B4:B11)	=count(mathsresults)

Tip: Excel doesn't allow spaces in cell names or range names.

Spreadsheet Functions Assignment Eleven

Create a new spreadsheet workbook and enter data as shown in Table 2.28 on page 58. Enter functions in the shaded cells to complete the spreadsheet.

1. Assign the names **mathsresults** to B4:B11, **chemresults** to C4:C11 and **engresults** to D4:D11.

2. Calculate average, highest and lowest mark and number of exams using functions and range names.

Table 2.28

	A	B	C	D
1	Analysis of Exam Results			
2				
3		Maths	Chemistry	English
4	Tom Boyle	89	58	60
5	Mick Gavin	44	62	n.a.
6	William Treacy	53	73	88
7	Sharon Byrne	70	n.a.	43
8	Jaki McKay	66	n.a.	75
9	Derek McCormack	30	77	78
10	Eileen Nolan	24	68	62
11	Margaret O Connell	59	91	68
12				
13	Average Mark			
14	Highest Mark			
15	Lowest Mark			
16	Number of Exams			

 Tip: When writing a formula or function that refers to named cells or ranges, press F3 to display a list of all cell and range names in your spreadsheet.

3. Format the averages to display zero decimal places.
4. Format headings to bold and align data as shown above.
5. Save the spreadsheet as **Analysis of Exam Results**.

Toolbar Buttons Introduced in Chapter Two

This button can be used to copy the format from one cell or range of cells to another cell or range or cells. Select the cell or range of cells that contains the

Figure 2.8 The **Format Painter** button

formatting you want to copy. Click the Format Painter button. The formats will be copied to the next cell or range of cells you highlight. Double clicking the Format Painter allows you to copy formats to multiple ranges.

Summary of Functions

Table 2.29

Function Name	Purpose	Example
SUM	Adding	=sum(B4:B15)
AVERAGE	Calculates average	=average(B4:B15)
MAX	Finds highest number	=max(B4:B15)
MIN	Finds lowest number	=min(B4:B15)
COUNT	Counts cells containing numbers	=count(B4:B15)
COUNTA	Counts cells that are not empty	=counta(A4:A15)
POWER	Raises a number to a power	=power(A2,10)
SQRT	Calculates square root	=sqrt(A2/3.14)
DB	Calculates depreciation using the declining balance method	=db($E$1,$E$2,$E$3,1)
SUMIF	Adds cell values in a range if they satisfy a given condition	=sumif(B4:B12,"Apples",E4:E12)
COUNTIF	Counts the number of cells in a range that satisfy a given condition	=countif(C4:C11,A14)

3

Naming and Linking Worksheets

In Chapter 3, you will learn how to

* Name and copy worksheets
* Create formulas to read data from multiple worksheets
* Create formulas linked to cells in multiple worksheets.

Naming Worksheets

An Excel workbook normally consists of 16 worksheets, a bit like a copybook with 16 pages. Excel names the worksheets Sheet1, Sheet2, Sheet3 and so on. By renaming a worksheet, it becomes easier to see at a glance what type of information that worksheet contains.

To rename Sheet1, point at Sheet1 with the mouse and then right click.

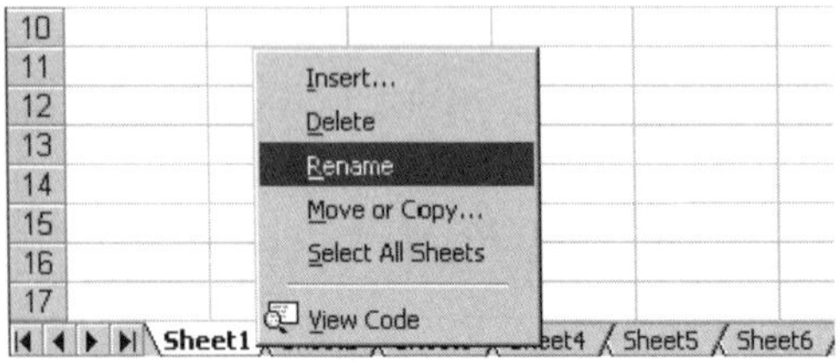

10						
11		Insert...				
12		Delete				
13		Rename				
14						
15		Move or Copy...				
16		Select All Sheets				
17						

Sheet1 ... eet4 / Sheet5 / Sheet6

Figure 3.1

Select Rename from the menu, type in the new name (in this case, Home Budget) for Sheet1 and press Enter. The name of Sheet1 changes to Home Budget, as shown below.

Home Budget / Sheet2 / Sheet3

Ready

Figure 3.2

Tip: All 16 worksheets are rarely required. Change the number of worksheets included in each new workbook by selecting Tools from the menu. Now select Options and click the General tab. Change Sheets in new workbook to four. In future all new workbooks that you create will have four worksheets. For spreadsheet users who need more than four worksheets, up to 255 worksheets can be included in each spreadsheet workbook.

Linking Worksheets in a Workbook

Organising data on different worksheets, instead of having a lot of data in a single worksheet, can make a spreadsheet easier to use and easier to understand. In the following example, we will see how data relating to the sale of raffle tickets contained in three separate worksheets can be summarised in a fourth worksheet. There are three ticket sellers: Jaki, Ian and Geraldine. A separate worksheet is used to record each ticket seller's sales.

	A	B	C	D	E
1	Sales of Raffle Tickets by:		Jaki		
2					
3		Week 1	Week 2	Week 3	Total
4	No. of Tickets	56	32	25	113
5					

I◄ ◄ ► ►I \ Jaki / Ian / Geraldine / Summary / I◄I

Figure 3.3

Data relating to Jaki has been entered in Sheet1, as shown above. Sheet1 has been renamed as Jaki.

	A	B	C	D	E
1	Sales of Raffle Tickets by:		Ian		
2					
3		Week 1	Week 2	Week 3	Total
4	No. of Tickets	45	24	30	99
5					

I◄ ◄ ► ►I \ Jaki \ Ian / Geraldine / Summary / I◄I

Figure 3.4

Sheet2 has been renamed as Ian and data relating to Ian's ticket sales has been entered, as shown above.

	A	B	C	D	E
1	Sales of Raffle Tickets by:		Geraldine		
2					
3		Week 1	Week 2	Week 3	Total
4	No. of Tickets	70	41	38	149
5					

I◄ ◄ ► ►I \ Jaki / Ian \ Geraldine / Summary / I◄I

Figure 3.5

The third worksheet contains data relating to Geraldine's ticket sales and this sheet has been renamed as Geraldine.

The fourth worksheet, which has been renamed as Summary, contains formulas that link to each individual ticket seller's name. It also contains formulas that

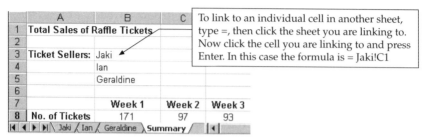

	A	B	C	To link to an individual cell in another sheet, type =, then click the sheet you are linking to. Now click the cell you are linking to and press Enter. In this case the formula is = Jaki!C1
1	Total Sales of Raffle Tickets			
2				
3	Ticket Sellers:	Jaki		
4		Ian		
5		Geraldine		
6				
7		Week 1	Week 2	Week 3
8	No. of Tickets	171	97	93

Jaki / Ian / Geraldine \ Summary

Figure 3.6

calculate the number of tickets sold in week one, week two and week three. Each of these formulas must refer to numbers stored in the three different worksheets to calculate the number of tickets sold.

	A	B
3	Ticket Sellers:	=Jaki!C1
4		=Ian!C1
5		=Geraldine!C1
6		
7		Week 1
8	No. of Tickets	=Jaki!B4+Ian!B4+Geraldine!B4
9		

Jaki / Ian / Geraldine \ Summary

Figure 3.7

Displayed above are formulas to link back to the individual ticket seller's names and a formula to calculate the number of tickets for week one.

Calculating Number of Tickets for Week One

1. Position the cell pointer in B8 of the Summary worksheet.
2. Type =, click the worksheet named Jaki, then click cell B4.
3. Type +, click the worksheet named Ian, then click cell B4.
4. Type +, click the worksheet named Geraldine, then click cell B4.
5. Press Enter (*NB: don't click the worksheet named Summary at this point*).

The resulting formula is as follows:

=Jaki!B4+Ian!B4+Geraldine!B4

Note: This formula can also be typed directly into the spreadsheet. At this stage it's easier to create the formula by selecting cells in different worksheets.

As well as referring to cells, the formula also refers to worksheets. =Jaki!B4 means cell B4 in the worksheet named Jaki. Notice how each worksheet name is followed by an exclamation mark.

Copying Worksheets

In a workbook containing many worksheets that are similar in structure, copying and then amending an existing worksheet is often quicker than creating a new worksheet from scratch. To copy a worksheet right click the worksheet name, as shown below.

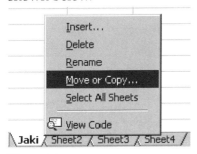

Figure 3.8

1. Select Move or Copy from the menu. The following dialog box is displayed.

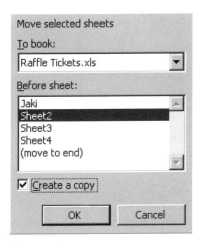

Figure 3.9

2. Click Create a copy and select Sheet2. This means that a copy of the worksheet called Jaki will be inserted before Sheet2. Excel assigns the name Jaki(2) to this worksheet. It can be renamed by right clicking the worksheet name and selecting Rename from the menu.

 Tip: You can also copy a worksheet by dragging the sheet tab of the worksheet you are copying and dropping it on another sheet tab while holding down the CTRL key.

Linking Worksheets Assignment One

Create a new spreadsheet workbook and enter the data shown in Table 3.1 in Sheet1. Enter formulas and functions in the shaded cells to complete the spreadsheet.

Table 3.1

	A	B	C	D	E	F
1	Travel Expenses		Joe Murphy			
2		Mileage a.m.	Mileage p.m.	Distance Travelled	Rate per Mile	Total Due
3	04/10/03	25109	25271		0.85	
4	05/10/03		25388		0.85	
5	06/10/03		25529		0.85	
6	07/10/03		25701		0.85	
7	08/10/03		25853		0.85	
8						
9			Total			

Tip: Dates can be copied using the fill handle. Enter 04/10/03 and drag the fill handle downwards to enter the remaining dates. This only works when the dates are in sequence.

1. Rename Sheet1 as Joe Murphy.
2. In B4 use a formula to read the mileage p.m. of the previous day. Copy this formula to B5, B6 and B7.
3. Calculate the distance travelled and the total due.
4. Use the SUM function to calculate the total distance travelled and overall total due.
5. Rename Sheet2 as Sile O Shea.
6. Enter the data shown in Table 3.2 on page 65 in the worksheet named Sile O Shea (*you could also copy the worksheet named Joe Murphy and then change the employee name and the mileage figures*).
7. Calculate mileage a.m., distance travelled and total due for Sile O Shea.
8. Rename Sheet3 as Tom Doyle.
9. Enter the data shown in Table 3.3 on page 65 in the worksheet named Tom Doyle (*or copy and amend an existing worksheet*).
10. Calculate mileage a.m., distance travelled and total due for Tom Doyle.
11. Rename Sheet4 as travel summary.
12. Enter the data shown in Table 3.4 on page 66 in the worksheet named Travel Summary.

Table 3.2

	A	B	C	D	E	F
1	Travel Expenses		Sile O Shea			
2		Mileage a.m.	Mileage p.m.	Distance Travelled	Rate per Mile	Total Due
3	04/10/03	73109	73215		0.85	
4	05/10/03		73399		0.85	
5	06/10/03		73501		0.85	
6	07/10/03		73546		0.85	
7	08/10/03		73722		0.85	
8						
9			Total			

Table 3.3

	A	B	C	D	E	F
1	Travel Expenses		Tom Doyle			
2		Mileage a.m.	Mileage p.m.	Distance Travelled	Rate per Mile	Total Due
3	04/10/03	59115	59209		0.85	
4	05/10/03		59356		0.85	
5	06/10/03		59592		0.85	
6	07/10/03		59771		0.85	
7	08/10/03		59920		0.85	
8						
9			Total			

13. Enter linking formulas in the shaded cells to read the employee name, distance travelled and total due from each of the three employee worksheets.

14. Format money amounts to currency in all worksheets.

15. Format headings to bold and align data, as shown.

16. Adjust column widths where necessary.

17. Print all worksheets.

18. Save the spreadsheet as **Travel Expenses**.

Table 3.4

	A	B	C
1	Summary of Travel Expenses		
2			
3	Employee Name	Distance Travelled	Total Due
4			
5			
6			

 Linking Worksheets Assignment Two

Create a new spreadsheet workbook and enter the data shown in
Table 3.5 on page 67 in Sheet1. Enter functions in the shaded cells to
complete the spreadsheet.

 Tip: Ensure that Autocomplete is turned on to speed up the entering of
results. From the menu select **Tools**, followed by **Options**. Click the Edit
tab and ensure that 'Enable Autocomplete for cell values' is on. When
Autocomplete is on Excel will suggest the remaining letters of a particular
result as soon as you type the first letter, as long as that result has already been
entered in column B. Excel's suggestion can be accepted by pressing Enter. For
example, when entering the second result type M, and Excel displays Merit in the
current cell. Press Enter to accept Excel's suggestion.

1. Rename Sheet1 as Spreadsheet Results.
2. Assign the name **spreadsheetresults** to the range B4:B25.
3. Use the COUNTIF function, together with the range name **spreadsheetresults**,
to count the number of distinctions, merits, passes and fails. (**Tip**: Use F3 to paste
the cell name into the function.).
4. Use the COUNTA function to count the number of students.
5. Highlight the range A3:B25 and select Format, Autoformat, Colorful1.
6. Highlight the range D3:E7 and select Format, Autoformat, Classic3.

 Tip: Holding down SHIFT and then pressing an arrow key is another
way of highlighting cells in a spreadsheet. This is particularly useful
when the highlighted range extends beyond one screen.

7. Rename Sheet2 as Database Results.
8. Enter the data shown in Table 3.6 on page 68 in the worksheet
named Database Results. (**Tip**: *Copy the student names from the Spreadsheet Results
worksheet.*)
9. Assign the name **databaseresults** to the range B4:B21.

Table 3.5

	A	B	C	D	E
1	**Spreadsheets Results**				
2					
3	**Student Name**	**Result**		**No of Distinctions**	
4	Tom Boyle	Merit		**No of Merits**	
5	Mick Gavin	Merit		**No of Passes**	
6	William Treacy	Pass		**No of Fails**	
7	Sharon Byrne	Merit		**Total Students**	
8	Jaki McKay	Distinction			
9	Derek McCormack	Fail			
10	Eileen Nolan	Merit			
11	Margaret O Connell	Distinction			
12	Dermot Rogers	Pass			
13	John Keegan	Merit			
14	Mary Hamilton	Merit			
15	Laura Sheehy	Merit			
16	Joe Dalton	Distinction			
17	Aileen Curtin	Merit			
18	Michael Finnegan	Fail			
19	Kay McKee	Distinction			
20	Paul O Gorman	Merit			
21	Brian Kelleher	Merit			
22	Frank O Brien	Merit			
23	Trish Rohan	Merit			
24	Philip McCullagh	Merit			
25	Andrew Winters	Distinction			

Table 3.6

	A	B	C	D	E
1	Database Results				
2					
3	Student Name	Result		No of Distinctions	
4	Tom Boyle	Merit		No of Merits	
5	Mick Gavin	Merit		No of Passes	
6	William Treacy	Pass		No of Fails	
7	Sharon Byrne	Merit		Total Students	
8	Jaki McKay	Distinction			
9	Derek McCormack	Fail			
10	Eileen Nolan	Merit			
11	Margaret O Connell	Distinction			
12	Dermot Rogers	Pass			
13	John Keegan	Merit			
14	Mary Hamilton	Merit			
15	Laura Sheehy	Merit			
16	Joe Dalton	Distinction			
17	Aileen Curtin	Merit			
18	Michael Finnegan	Pass			
19	Kay McKee	Distinction			
20	Paul O Gorman	Merit			
21	Brian Kelleher	Merit			

10. Use the COUNTIF function, together with the range name databaseresults, to count the number of distinctions, merits, passes and fails.

11. Use the COUNTA function to count the number of students.

12. Use Autoformat as before.

13. Rename Sheet3 as Word Processing Results.

14. Enter the data shown in Table 3.7 on page 69 in the worksheet named Word Processing Results.

15. Assign the name **wordprocessingresults** to the range B4:B28.

16. Use the COUNTIF function, together with the range name **wordprocessingresults**, to count the number of distinctions, merits, passes and fails.

Table 3.7

	A	B	C	D	E
1	**Word Processing Results**				
2					
3	**Student Name**	**Result**		**No of Distinctions**	
4	Tom Boyle	Distinction		**No of Merits**	
5	Mick Gavin	Merit		**No of Passes**	
6	William Treacy	Merit		**No of Fails**	
7	Sharon Byrne	Pass		**Total Students**	
8	Jaki McKay	Merit			
9	Derek McCormack	Merit			
10	Eileen Nolan	Distinction			
11	Margaret O Connell	Pass			
12	Dermot Rogers	Merit			
13	John Keegan	Merit			
14	Mary Hamilton	Merit			
15	Laura Sheehy	Merit			
16	Joe Dalton	Distinction			
17	Aileen Curtin	Pass			
18	Michael Finnegan	Merit			
19	Kay McKee	Merit			
20	Paul O Gorman	Pass			
21	Brian Kelleher	Merit			
22	Frank O Brien	Distinction			
23	Trish Rohan	Merit			
24	Philip McCullagh	Distinction			
25	Andrew Winters	Distinction			
26	Eamon Staunton	Merit			
27	Declan Mulligan	Distinction			
28	Nuala McInerney	Merit			

17. Use the COUNTA function to count the number of students.
18. Use Autoformat as before.
19. Rename Sheet4 as Summary.
20. Enter the data shown in Table 3.8 in the worksheet named Summary.

Table 3.8

	A	B	C	D
1	Exam Report			
2				
3		Spreadsheets	Database	Word Processing
4	Distinction			
5	Merit			
6	Pass			
7	Fail			
8	Total Students			

21. Enter formulas to link to the relevant cells in the Spreadsheet Results, Database Results and Word Processing Results worksheets.
22. Format the range A3:D8 using Autoformat, Classic3.
23. Save the spreadsheet as **Computer Applications Results**.

 Linking Worksheets Assignment Three

Create a new spreadsheet workbook and enter the data shown in Table 3.9 on page 71 in Sheet1. Enter functions in the shaded cells to complete the spreadsheet.

Tip: Weekdays can be copied using the fill handle. Enter Monday and drag the fill handle downwards to enter the remaining days. This only works when the days are in sequence.

1. Rename Sheet1 as 0745.
2. Calculate total ticket sales at each station.
3. Calculate the grand total for ticket sales.
4. Rename Sheet2 as 1100.

Table 3.9

	A	B	C	D	E	F	G	H
1	Week 1 Ticket Sales							
2	Galway-Dublin departing 07:45							
3								
4		Galway	Athenry	Ballinasloe	Athlone	Tullamore	Portarlington	Kildare
5	Monday	233	48	64	104	96	71	180
6	Tuesday	172	23	39	81	95	57	148
7	Wednesday	130	18	36	72	81	59	137
8	Thursday	163	18	35	71	80	47	152
9	Friday	220	21	51	81	100	75	180
10								
11	Total Ticket Sales							
12								
13	Grand Total							

Table 3.10

	A	B	C	D	E	F	G	H
1	Week 1 Ticket Sales							
2	Galway-Dublin departing 11:00							
3								
4		Galway	Athenry	Ballinasloe	Athlone	Tullamore	Portarlington	Kildare
5	Monday	65	12	20	34	28	20	45
6	Tuesday	49	6	18	28	30	18	31
7	Wednesday	34	4	13	22	25	16	30
8	Thursday	42	5	10	18	23	18	34
9	Friday	81	4	13	23	29	19	40
10								
11	Total Ticket Sales							
12								
13	Grand Total							

5. Enter the data shown in Table 3.10 on page 71 in the worksheet named 1100 (or copy and amend the 0745 worksheet).
6. Calculate total ticket sales and grand total as before.
7. Rename Sheet3 as 1510.
8. Enter the data shown in Table 3.11 below in the worksheet named 1510.
9. Calculate total ticket sales and grand total as before.
10. Rename Sheet4 as Weekly Ticket Sales.
11. Enter the data shown in Table 3.12 on page 73 in the worksheet named Weekly Ticket Sales.
12. Calculate total weekly ticket sales for each day at each station using formulas which add data from the 0745, 1100 and 1510 worksheets.
13. Calculate total ticket sales and grand total as before.
14. Save the spreadsheet as **Ticket Sales Galway-Dublin Route**.

Table 3.11

	A	B	C	D	E	F	G	H
1	Week 1 Ticket Sales							
2	Galway-Dublin departing 15:10							
3								
4		Galway	Athenry	Ballinasloe	Athlone	Tullamore	Portarlington	Kildare
5	Monday	56	15	12	15	28	25	50
6	Tuesday	43	5	6	10	30	20	45
7	Wednesday	31	6	2	12	25	22	37
8	Thursday	25	8	8	8	23	15	42
9	Friday	34	10	10	20	29	35	67
10								
11	Total Ticket Sales							
12								
13	Grand Total							

Table 3.12

	A	B	C	D	E	F	G	H
1	Week 1 Ticket Sales Summary							
2	07:45, 11:00 and 15:10 Trains							
3								
4		Galway	Athenry	Ballinasloe	Athlone	Tullamore	Portarlington	Kildare
5	Monday							
6	Tuesday							
7	Wednesday							
8	Thursday							
9	Friday							
10								
11	Total Ticket Sales							
12								
13	Grand Total							

4

Spreadsheet Charts

In Chapter 4, you will learn how to

- Create column charts, bar charts, line charts, pie charts and XY charts
- Modify existing charts to include new data.

Using Charts in a Spreadsheet

Presenting information graphically helps the recipient of the information to grasp the meaning of it more quickly and to remember it more easily.
It's difficult to figure out the trends by looking at the information contained in Table 4.1. By charting this information, we can make it much easier to understand.

Table 4.1

	A	B	C	D	E	F	G
1	Distance Travelled						
2		Jan	Feb	Mar	Apr	May	Jun
3	Jim	1175	1298	875	901	809	900
4	Tom	2012	1899	790	855	750	800
5	Eileen	500	560	555	1990	2025	2117
6	Karen	408	459	501	2339	2450	2098

Looking at the chart in Figure 4.1 on page 75, we can instantly see that Eileen and Karen do most of their travelling in April, May and June. Tom does most of his travelling in January and February and Jim's travel is more or less constant.

There is a wide range of chart types available to spreadsheet users. The most popular chart types are column, bar, line, pie and XY. Column, bar, line and pie charts will be illustrated using the above information relating to employee travel. The XY chart type will be illustrated using test results from a speed experiment.

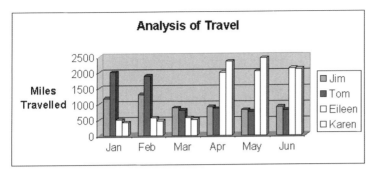

Figure 4.1

Types of Spreadsheet Chart

Column Chart (Single Series)

In a column chart, each number is represented by a vertical column. The higher the number, the higher the column. The set of numbers that the chart is representing is called the data series. In Table 4.2 there is only one set of numbers so the chart displayed below has only one column for each month. From the chart in Figure 4.2, we can quickly see that February was Jim's busiest month for travelling.

Table 4.2

	A	B	C	D	E	F	G	
1	Distance Travelled							1 data series
2		Jan	Feb	Mar	Apr	May	Jun	
3	Jim	1175	1298	875	901	809	900	

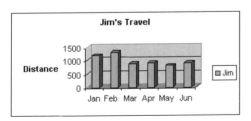

Figure 4.2

Column Chart (Multiple Series)

This type of chart is useful if we want to show the relationship between different sets of numbers.

In Figure 4.3 on page 76, the chart is representing four sets of numbers

Table 4.3

	A	B	C	D	E	F	G	
1	Distance Travelled							4 data series
2		Jan	Feb	Mar	Apr	May	Jun	
3	Jim	1175	1298	875	901	809	900	
4	Tom	2012	1899	790	855	750	800	
5	Eileen	500	560	555	1990	2025	2117	
6	Karen	408	459	501	2339	2450	2098	

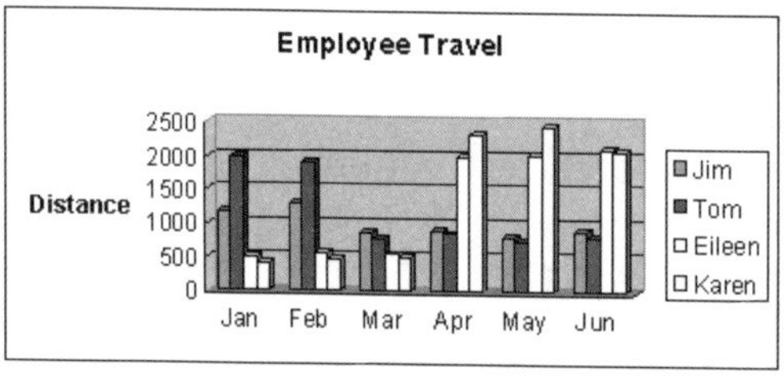

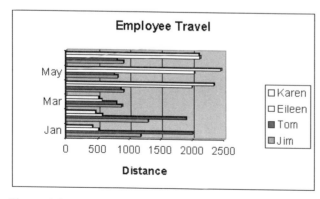

Figure 4.3

(Jim's travel, Tom's travel, Eileen's travel and Karen's travel). Each month has four columns. A different colour is used for each employee's column. With this type of chart, we can make comparisons between distances travelled by employees in a given month as well as seeing the trend of each employee's travel over a six-month period.

Bar Chart

In a bar chart, each number is represented by a horizontal bar. This places more emphasis on values and less emphasis on time, as seen in Figure 4.4.

Figure 4.4

Stacked Bar Chart

A stacked bar chart allows us to see at a glance what percentage of the total monthly travel each employee accounted for.

From the chart in Figure 4.5, we quickly see that Karen accounted for a small portion of the total travel in January, February and March but accounted for a much higher portion in April, May and June.

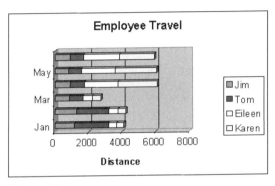

Figure 4.5

Line Chart

In a line chart, each number in a data series is represented by a dot. The higher the number, the higher the dot. The dots are joined to form a line, which fluctuates according to the distance travelled. Each employee has a different coloured line. Line charts are useful if you want to compare values at a given point in time.

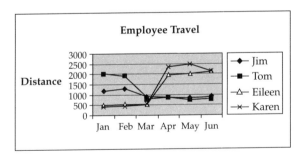

Figure 4.6

Pie Chart

A pie chart only shows one data series. It's useful when we want to focus on a particular employee, in this case Karen, and allows us to see which months Karen did most of her travelling in and which months were the quietest. The pie chart also calculates the percentage of the total made up by each slice of the pie.

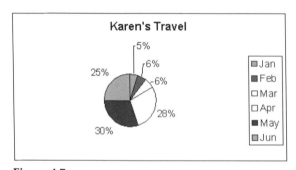

Figure 4.7

Separate pie charts could also be created for Jim, Tom, and Eileen.

XY Chart

An XY chart shows the relationships among the numeric values in two or more data series. It's commonly used in scientific applications, such as displaying the results of an experiment.

The example in Figure 4.8 shows how actual speed recorded during a test compares with the speed that was predicted before the test was carried out.

Table 4.4

	A	*B*	*C*
1	Elapsed Time (secs)	Speed (mph)	Predicted Speed (mph)
2	1	13	17
3	2	17	23
4	3	26	31
5	4	37	44
6	5	51	56
7	6	60	65

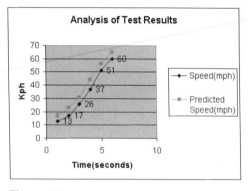

Figure 4.8

We can see from these examples that there are many ways of graphically presenting a particular set of data. The method you choose depends on the type of message you want to get across.

How to Create a Chart

We'll learn how to create a chart using a practical example. Create a new spreadsheet workbook and enter data as shown in Table 4.5.

Table 4.5

	A	B	C	D	E
1	Yearly Sales				
2		2000	2001	2002	2003
3	West Region	100000	125000	112000	130000
4	South Region	80000	85000	90000	70000
5	East Region	112000	100000	120000	114000

1. Select the cells that contain the data you want to appear in the chart, as shown in Figure 4.9.

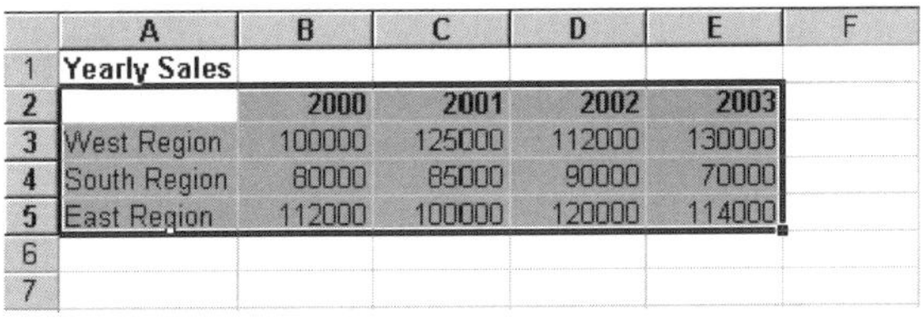

	A	B	C	D	E	F
1	Yearly Sales					
2		2000	2001	2002	2003	
3	West Region	100000	125000	112000	130000	
4	South Region	80000	85000	90000	70000	
5	East Region	112000	100000	120000	114000	
6						
7						

Figure 4.9

Rule one: There should be no blank rows or blank columns in the highlighted area.

Rule two: The highlighted area should only contain the numbers that create the chart together with one row of headings and one column of headings.

2. Click the chart wizard button, as shown in Figure 4.10.

Chart Wizard button

Figure 4.10

3. Column Chart is already selected. Click Next to accept this.

4. You are now asked whether your data series is arranged in rows or columns. If you select rows the chart wizard will create a vertical column for each row of numbers in the range highlighted in step one, excluding the year headings. This results in three columns per year representing west region, south region and east region, as shown below.

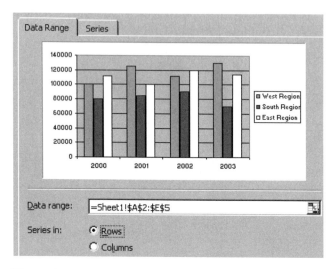

Figure 4.11

If you select Columns the chart wizard will create a vertical column for each column of numbers in the range highlighted in step one, excluding the year headings. This results in four columns per region representing the years 2000, 2001, 2002 and 2003, as shown below.

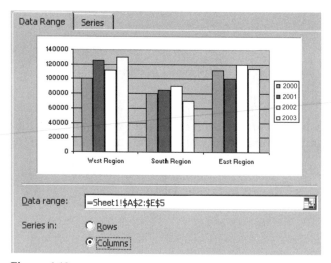

Figure 4.12

In this case, we will set up the series in rows. Select Rows and click Next.

5. Enter the main chart title together with the labels for the x axis and y axis, as shown below (the x axis is the horizontal line at the bottom of the graph. The y axis is the vertical line at the left of the graph). Click Next when you've finished entering the titles and labels.

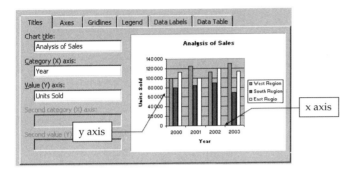

Figure 4.13

6. You're now asked whether you want the chart as an object in the spreadsheet (this means that the chart will be displayed on the same page as your data) or as a separate sheet, known as a chart sheet (this means that the chart and the data will be on different sheets). Select 'As object' in Sheet1 and click Finish.

Tip: In cases where 'separate sheet' is selected, it's a good idea to enter a name for the new chart sheet at this point.

The chart is now displayed on the same worksheet as the data that was used to create the chart. It graphically represents data entered in the range A2:E5. If data in this range is edited, the changes will automatically be reflected in the chart.

7. Save the spreadsheet as **Chart Example**.

Charts – Important Terms

Data Series

The data series is the set of numbers the spreadsheet needs to create a chart. A chart can have one or many data series. In the example in Figure 4.14, there are

	A	B	C	D	E	F
1	Yearly Sales					
2		2000	2001	2002	2003	
3	West Region	100000	125000	112000	130000	
4	South Region	80000	85000	90000	70000	
5	East Region	112000	100000	120000	114000	
6						
7						

West Region Series B3:E3

South Region Series B4:E4

East Region Series B5:E5

Figure 4.14

three data series: west region, south region and east region. Excel assumes that the first column and the first row of the highlighted area are titles or descriptions. The remainder of the highlighted area contains the numbers that create the chart. Excel interprets these numbers as being rows of data if 'Series in rows' is selected or columns of data if 'Series in columns' is selected.

Value (Y) Axis

This is text that describes the values on the y axis (the vertical line on the left of the chart).

Category (X) Axis

This is text that describes the labels on the x axis (the horizontal line at the bottom of the chart).

Legend

If there is more than one data series in the chart, a different colour is used for each series. The legend usually appears at the side of the chart and shows the colour of each data series, i.e. the west region is blue, the south region is wine and the east region is yellow.

Chart Title

The chart title is displayed above the chart.

Data Labels

This option allows you to display values for each data series.

Data Table

If you choose this option, the data from the spreadsheet is attached to the graph.

Chart Sheet

A chart sheet is a separate sheet within a workbook that displays a chart but doesn't store any data. Chart sheets are very useful if you require a greater level of

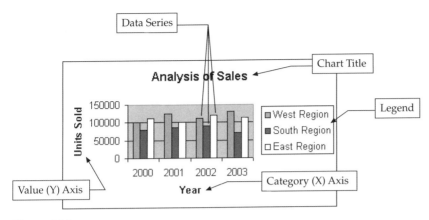

Figure 4.15

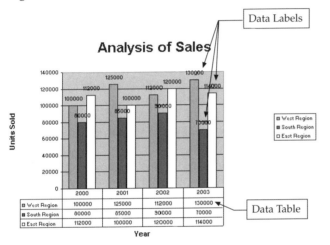

Figure 4.16

detail in your chart or if you don't have enough room to include your chart in the worksheet that contains the source data.

Spreadsheet Charts Assignment One

Create a new spreadsheet workbook and enter the data shown in Table 4.6 on page 84 in Sheet1.

For questions two, three and four use the chart title Exam Results 2003.

1. Rename Sheet1 as Exam Data.
2. Display the data using a column chart (where each result is represented by a column). The title for the x axis is Subject. The title for the y axis is No. of Students. The chart should be on a separate chart sheet named Overall 2003 (Column).
3. Display the data using a bar chart (where each subject is represented by a bar). The title for the x axis is Result. The title for the y axis is No. of Students. The chart should be on a separate chart sheet named Overall 2003 (Bar).

Table 4.6

	A	B	C	D	E
1	Exam Results 2003				
2		Fail	Pass	Merit	Distinction
3	Spreadsheets	2	5	25	8
4	Database	1	2	15	20
5	Word Processing	0	6	30	20

4. Display the data using a line chart (where each subject is represented by a line). The title for the x axis is Result. The title for the y axis is No. of Students. The chart should be on a separate chart sheet named Overall 2003 (Line).

5. Display the spreadsheets results using a pie chart. The chart title is Spreadsheets – Breakdown of Grades. Click the Data Labels tab and show the percentage represented by each slice of the pie. Display the pie chart on the same worksheet as the data.

6. Display the database results using a pie chart.

Note: You'll have to highlight two separate ranges to do this.

The chart title is Database – Breakdown of Grades. Show the percentage represented by each slice of the pie. Display the pie chart on the same worksheet as the data.

Tip: You can select multiple spreadsheet ranges by highlighting the first range as normal and then holding down CTRL and dragging with the mouse to highlight subsequent ranges.

7. Display the word processing results using a pie chart.

Note: You'll have to highlight two separate ranges to do this.

The chart title is Word Processing – Breakdown of Grades. Show the percentage represented by each slice of the pie. Display the pie chart on the same worksheet as the data.

8. An error was made when recording the Word Processing Results. Five students failed this subject. Update the spreadsheet and check that this change has been reflected in all charts that display word processing results.

9. Print preview the Exam Data worksheet. If necessary, move and resize the pie charts so that the data and the charts fit on one printed page.

10. Print the Exam Data worksheet.

11. Save the spreadsheet as **Exam Results 2003**.

Additional Points Concerning Pie Charts

To create a pie chart, we need to highlight one row of headings and one row of data. This is straightforward if the headings and the data are next to each other, as shown in Figure 4.17 (where we are creating a pie chart for spreadsheets).

	A	B	C	D	E	F
1	Exam Results 2003					
2		Fail	Pass	Merit	Distinction	
3	Spreadsheets	2	5	25	8	
4	Database	1	2	15	20	
5	Word Processing	0	6	30	20	
6						
7						

Figure 4.17

The range A2:E3, displayed in Figure 4.17, can be highlighted by clicking and dragging with the mouse.

Area to be Highlighted for Database Pie Chart

Where the headings and data aren't next to each other we need to highlight separate ranges, as shown below. This is done by highlighting the headings, then holding down the CTRL key and highlighting the data.

	A	B	C	D	E	F
1	Exam Results 2003					
2		Fail	Pass	Merit	Distinction	
3	Spreadsheets	2	5	25	8	
4	Database	1	2	15	20	
5	Word Processing	0	6	30	20	
6						
7						

Figure 4.18

First highlight A2:E2, then hold down the CTRL key and highlight A4:E4.

Tip: Both highlighted areas must contain the same number of cells. For this reason, A2 must be included in the first highlighted range even though it doesn't contain any data. The pie chart will be incorrect if both highlighted ranges don't contain the same number of cells.

A word of warning: if A2:E4 is highlighted when creating a database pie chart, as shown below, the numbers in the first series (i.e. spreadsheets) will be used to create the chart.

	A	B	C	D	E	F
1	Exam Results 2003					
2		Fail	Pass	Merit	Distinction	
3	Spreadsheets	2	5	25	8	
4	Database	1	2	15	20	
5	Word Processing	0	6	30	20	
6						
7						

Figure 4.19

A pie chart created from the range highlighted above will be based on the spreadsheets exam results and not on the database exam results.

Area to be Highlighted for Word Processing Pie Chart

First highlight A2:E2, then hold down the CTRL key and highlight A5:E5.

	A	B	C	D	E	F
1	Exam Results 2003					
2		Fail	Pass	Merit	Distinction	
3	Spreadsheets	2	5	25	8	
4	Database	1	2	15	20	
5	Word Processing	0	6	30	20	
6						
7						

Figure 4.20

Adding Additional Data to a Chart

If you add data to your spreadsheet after the chart has been created, this can be included in the chart by adjusting the source data of the chart.

1. If your chart is on the same worksheet as the data, make sure the chart is selected. If your chart is on a separate chart sheet, display that chart sheet.

2. Select Chart from the menu and then select Source Data. Shown in Figure 4.21 is the source data from the bar chart created in assignment one.

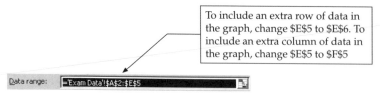

To include an extra row of data in the graph, change $E$5 to $E$6. To include an extra column of data in the graph, change $E$5 to $F$5

Data range: ='Exam Data'!$A$2:$E$5

Figure 4.21

3. To include an additional row of data in the graph, increase the row number of the second cell reference by one (in the example $E$5 would be changed to $E$6).

4. To include an additional column of data in the graph, change the column letter of the second cell reference to the next letter in the alphabet (in the example $E$5 would be changed to $F$5).

Spreadsheet Charts Assignment Two

Create a new spreadsheet workbook and enter the data shown in Table 4.7 in Sheet1.

Table 4.7

	A	B	C	D	E
1	Analysis of Educational Outcomes 2003				
2					
3	Department	Further Education	CE Scheme	Employment	Other
4	Science	125	90	373	21
5	Business	86	106	329	47
6	Law	15	0	86	12
7	Agricultural	12	2	48	6

1. Rename Sheet1 as Data.
2. Display the above data using a column chart (where each outcome is represented by a column). The chart title is Analysis of Educational Outcomes 2003. The title for the x axis is Department and the title for the y axis is No. of Students. The chart should be on a separate chart sheet named 2003 Outcomes (Column). Print the 2003 Outcomes (Column) chart sheet.
3. Display the data using a bar chart (where each department is represented by a bar). The chart title is Analysis of Educational Outcomes 2003. The title for the x axis is Outcome and the title for the y axis is No. of Students. The chart should be on a separate chart sheet named 2003 Outcomes (Bar).
4. Display the outcomes of the science department using a pie chart. The chart title is Progression of Science Graduates 2003. Select the show label and percent option. Display the pie chart on a separate chart sheet named Science 2003.
5. Display the outcomes of the business department using a pie chart. The chart title is Progression of Business Graduates 2003. Select the show label and percent option. Display the pie chart on a separate chart sheet named Business 2003.
6. Display the outcomes of the law department using a pie chart. The chart title is Progression of Law Graduates 2003. Select the show label and percent option. Display the pie chart on a separate chart sheet named Law 2003.
7. Display the outcomes of the agricultural department using a pie chart. The chart title is Progression of Agricultural Graduates 2003. Select the show label and percent option. Display the pie chart on a separate chart sheet named Agricultural 2003.
8. Enter new data relating to the engineering department in row eight of the spreadsheet, as shown in Table 4.8. Include this new data in both the column and bar charts by adjusting the cell references of the source data.

Table 4.8

8	Engineering	25	1	250	15

9. Display the outcomes of the engineering department using a pie chart. The chart title is Progression of Engineering Graduates 2003. Select the show label and percent option. Display the pie chart on a separate chart sheet named Engineering 2003.

10. Save the spreadsheet as **Analysis of Educational Outcomes**.

 Spreadsheet Charts Assignment Three

Create a new spreadsheet workbook and enter the data shown in Table 4.9 in Sheet1.

Table 4.9

	A	B	C
1	Club Fundraising		
2		Target	Actual
3	January	2000	1800
4	February	5000	4200
5	March	8000	6950
6	April	12000	10250
7	May	16000	12870
8	June	20000	16250

1. Rename Sheet1 as Target vs Actual.
2. Format all numbers to currency, with zero decimal places.
3. Display the above data using an XY chart. The chart title is Club Fundraising. The title for the x axis is Months and the title for the y axis is Euros. The chart should be on the same worksheet as the data.
4. The actual figure for June was incorrectly recorded. It was actually €17500. Update the spreadsheet and check that this change has been reflected in the chart.
5. Save the spreadsheet as **Fundraising**.

 Spreadsheet Charts Assignment Four

Create a new spreadsheet workbook and enter the data shown in Table 4.10 on page 89 in Sheet1.

1. Rename Sheet1 as Passenger Data.
2. Display the data using a line chart (where each destination is represented by a line). The chart title is Analysis of Passenger Numbers. The title for the y axis is No. of Passengers. The chart should be on a separate chart sheet named Travel Graph.

Table 4.10

	A	B	C	D
1	Passenger Numbers			
2		Stranraer	Hollyhead	Le Havre
3	Monday	290	450	280
4	Tuesday	250	400	220
5	Wednesday	295	310	350
6	Thursday	300	490	210
7	Friday	400	550	450
8	Saturday	525	550	500
9	Sunday	480	400	520

3. Add the data for the Cairnryan route, as shown in Table 4.11, in column E of the spreadsheet. Include this new data in the chart by adjusting the cell references of the source data.

Table 4.11

E
Cairnryan
320
250
300
320
350
450
450

4. Save the spreadsheet as **Passenger Ferries**.

Creating a Column Chart Based on Multiple Ranges

When you're creating a chart sometimes the data will be in a number of non-adjacent ranges. When selecting multiple ranges, select the first range as normal with the mouse. To select additional ranges, hold down the CTRL key while dragging with the mouse.

Worked Example

1. Open the spreadsheet named Rock Café.

6								
7	Artist	Date	Stalls	%Full	Circle	%Full	Balcony	%Full
8	The Corrs	08/09/2003	150	50%	300	86%	220	88%
9	The Frames	10/09/2003	276	92%	245	70%	141	56%
10	Aslan	11/09/2003	290	97%	307	88%	209	84%
11	Jack L	14/09/2003	250	83%	312	89%	196	78%
12	Westlife	18/09/2003	300	100%	350	100%	250	100%
13	Ronan Keating	19/09/2003	100	33%	267	76%	233	93%
14	Brian Kennedy	20/09/2003	180	60%	255	73%	200	80%
15								

Figure 4.22

2. Select four separate ranges, as shown in Figure 4.22.
3. Create a column chart with the stalls, circle and balcony on the horizontal axis, where the number of tickets sold in each section at each concert is represented by a column. The chart title is Ticket Sales Analysis. The title for the y axis is Tickets Sold. The chart should be on a separate chart sheet named Sales Chart.
4. Click the Save button to save the spreadsheet.

Important Points Relating to Charts Based on Multiple Ranges

1. There should be a heading in the top cell of each range selected and the heading shouldn't occupy more than one cell.
2. Each selected range should contain the same number of cells. In the example in Figure 4.23, there would be an error in the graph because not all ranges selected contain the same number of cells.

7	Artist	Date	Stalls	%Full	Circle	%Full	Balcony
8	The Corrs	08/09/2003	150	50%	300	86%	220
9	The Frames	10/09/2003	276	92%	245	70%	141
10	Aslan	11/09/2003	290	97%	307	88%	209
11	Jack L	14/09/2003	250	83%	312	89%	196
12	Westlife	18/09/2003	300	100%	350	100%	250
13	Ronan Keating	19/09/2003	100	33%	267	76%	233
14	Brian Kennedy	20/09/2003	180	60%	255	73%	200
15							

Figure 4.23

3. The first range selected should contain headings or descriptions. These will be inserted either in the legend or below the horizontal axis depending on whether 'Series in rows' or 'Series in columns' is selected.

Toolbar Buttons Introduced in Chapter Four

Click this button to display the chart wizard, which helps you create a range of different charts by bringing you through a series of steps.

Figure 4.24   The **Chart Wizard** button

5

Sorting Spreadsheet Data

In Chapter 5 you will learn how to

- Sort spreadsheet data in ascending and descending order
- Use a custom sort for weekdays and month names
- Create your own custom sort.

Data such as customer transactions is often entered in a spreadsheet in the order in which it naturally occurs. You'll often want to view that data in a different order, such as in ascending order of customer name or descending order of amount owed. There are three main methods of sorting data in a spreadsheet, as outlined below.

1. **Numerical sort**: Numbers in a particular row or column can be rearranged in ascending (from the lowest to the highest number) or descending (from the highest to the lowest number) numerical order.

2. **Alphabetical sort**: Text, such as customer names, can be rearranged in ascending (starting with names that begin with a, b, c and ending with names that begin with x, y, z) or descending (starting with names that begin with x, y, z and ending with names that begin with a, b, c) alphabetical order.

3. **Custom sort**: If you can't get the data into the order you require using a numerical or alphabetical sort, Excel has a number of custom sorts. For example, if we were to sort the days of the week alphabetically, we would get Friday, Monday, Saturday, Sunday, Thursday, Tuesday, Wednesday. Custom sorts are available for day and month names.

Figure 5.1

Figure 5.2

The Sort Ascending and Sort Descending buttons can be used when sorting data based on one column.

Sorting Spreadsheet Data Based on One Column

Table 5.1

	A	B	C
1	Formula 1 Drivers Championship		
2			
3	Driver Name	Team	Points
4	Heidfeld	Sauber	2
5	Montoya	Williams	17
6	Raikkonen	McLaren	4
7	Button	Renault	8
8	Salo	Toyota	2
9	Webber	Minardi	2
10	Schumacher M	Ferrari	34
11	Coulthard	McLaren	5
12	Irvine	Jaguar	3
13	Massa	Sauber	1
14	Schumacher R	Williams	20
15	Barrichello	Ferrari	6

Data relating to Formula 1 drivers has been entered in the worksheet displayed in Table 5.1. The data isn't in any particular order. We will sort the data in descending order of points. This means that the driver with the most points will be at the top of the list and the driver with the least points will be at the bottom of the list.

1. Position the cell pointer in any cell containing data in column C (any cell in the range C4:C15).
2. Click the Sort Descending button on the toolbar. The data is rearranged as displayed in Table 5.2.

Table 5.2

	A	B	C
1	Formula 1 Drivers Championship		
2			
3	Driver Name	Team	Points
4	Schumacher M	Ferrari	34
5	Schumacher R	Williams	20
6	Montoya	Williams	17
7	Button	Renault	8
8	Barrichello	Ferrari	6
9	Coulthard	McLaren	5
10	Raikkonen	McLaren	4
11	Irvine	Jaguar	3
12	Heidfeld	Sauber	2
13	Salo	Toyota	2
14	Webber	Minardi	2
15	Massa	Sauber	1

 The data is now in descending order of points, as shown above. (**Note**: To see the data in ascending order of points, simply click the Sort Ascending button.)

Important: Don't highlight the column you're sorting before you click the Sort Ascending or Sort Descending button. This would result in data being sorted *only in the highlighted column,* causing your data to be mixed up.

 Sorting Spreadsheet Data Assignment One

Create a new spreadsheet workbook and enter the data shown in Table 5.3 on page 95 in Sheet1. Enter formulas in the shaded cells to complete the spreadsheet.

1. The adjusted score is the score minus handicap.
2. Under/over par is the adjusted score minus course par. (*Hint: Assign the name coursepar to cell B1 and then use this name in the formula.*)
3. Sort the data in ascending order of under/over par.
4. Print the spreadsheet.
5. Save the spreadsheet as **Leader Board**.

Table 5.3

	A	B	C	D	E
1	Course Par	72			
2					
3		Handicap	Score	Adjusted Score	Under/Over Par
4	Tiger Woods	6	76		
5	Paul McGinley	10	85		
6	Padraig Harrington	7	76		
7	Bernard Langer	10	84		
8	Seve Ballesterous	7	71		
9	Nick Faldo	8	81		
10	Paul Azinger	7	72		
11	Vijah Singh	11	78		
12	Colin Montgomerie	9	79		
13	Mark O Meara	12	82		

Sorting Spreadsheet Data Based on Two Columns

Returning to our Formula 1 spreadsheet we can see that because each Formula 1 team has two drivers, we can sort the data first in ascending order of team so that Ferrari is at the top of the list and Williams is at the bottom of the list. We can then sort in descending order of points so that, of the two Ferrari drivers, Schumacher M will be higher up in the list and of the two Williams drivers, Schumacher R will be higher up in the list.

To sort by two columns, we must access the Sort command by selecting Data from the menu.

1. Click in any cell in the data you are sorting (any cell in the range A4:C15). See Table 5.2 on page 94.

2. Select **Data**, followed by **Sort** from the menu (see Figure 5.3 on page 96).

3. Select team as the primary sort in ascending order. Select points as the secondary sort in descending order. The resulting order is displayed in Table 5.4 on page 96.

Sorting Spreadsheet Data – Important Points

1. Excel assumes that the first row of the range contains headings and doesn't include this row in the sort unless you select 'No header row'.

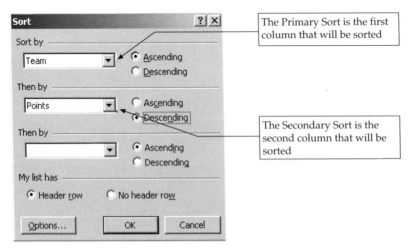

The Primary Sort is the first column that will be sorted

The Secondary Sort is the second column that will be sorted

Figure 5.3

Table 5.4

	A	B	C
1	**Formula 1 Drivers Championship**		
2			
3	**Driver Name**	**Team**	**Points**
4	Schumacher M	Ferrari	34
5	Barrichello	Ferrari	6
6	Irvine	Jaguar	3
7	Coulthard	McLaren	5
8	Raikkonen	McLaren	4
9	Webber	Minardi	2
10	Button	Renault	8
11	Heidfeld	Sauber	2
12	Massa	Sauber	1
13	Salo	Toyota	2
14	Schumacher R	Williams	20
15	Montoya	Williams	17

2. Don't include blank rows or columns in the range you're sorting. Excel won't include all of the data in the sort if this is the case.

3. When sorting by one column, don't highlight that column.

4. Each heading should occupy one cell only. This is because Excel assumes that the first row of the highlighted range contains headings. If headings are entered in two rows, the second row of headings will be sorted with the data.

5. If the column headings don't have a different format, e.g. bold, compared to the data in the list, Excel may include them in the sort.

Sorting Spreadsheet Data Assignment Two

Create a new spreadsheet workbook and enter the data shown in Table 5.5 in Sheet1. Enter formulas in the shaded cells to complete the spreadsheet.

Table 5.5

	A	B	C	D	E
1	Name	Department	Local Calls	International Calls	Total
2	John O Shea	Sales	46.85	103.47	
3	Paul Harris	Admin	38.21	0	
4	Jessica Dunne	Sales	29.09	89.83	
5	Aidan Murphy	Finance	54.88	0	
6	Donal Nesdale	Sales	37.36	0	
7	Paula Clane	Admin	61.22	0	
8	Mike Nicholls	Admin	50.84	0	
9	Joan Langton	Finance	46.04	0	
10	Maeve Rochford	Admin	33.97	0	
11	Mary Dunne	Finance	37.19	0	
12	Peter Byrne	Finance	73.47	0	
13	Tom Finn	Finance	61.07	0	
14	Tony Sheehan	Sales	55.59	208.56	
15	Michelle Cunningham	Sales	38.50	180.99	
16	Vicky Sullivan	Admin	43.21	23.41	

1. Calculate the total.

2. Sort the data first in ascending order of department and then in descending order of total.

3. Format all money amounts to currency.

4. Save the spreadsheet as **Telephone Charges by Department**.

Custom Sort Orders

Custom sorts are useful where we need to sort data in day or month order. Create a new spreadsheet workbook and enter the data shown in Table 5.6 in Sheet1.

Table 5.6

	A	B	C
1	Name	Department	Started
2	Niamh O Leary	Sales	March
3	Martin Hegarty	Computer	January
4	Liz Hartnett	Admin	May
5	Colin Dunne	Production	March
6	Liam O Looney	Production	February
7	Eileen Flaherty	Sales	April
8	Eamonn Dineen	Admin	March
9	Siobhan Tully	Computer	January
10	Vin Clarke	Production	April
11	Tom Evans	Computer	February
12	Sarah Mooney	Admin	March
13	Samantha Burke	Computer	May

1. Select any cell in the range A2:C13.
2. Select Data followed by Sort from the menu and then select Started from the 'Sort by' list.
3. Select Ascending and then click Options. Under 'First key sort order' select January, February, March, April.
4. Click OK twice to implement the sort.
5. Save the spreadsheet as **Personnel File**.

Creating Your Own Custom Sort Order

When we need to sort data in an order that isn't numerical, alphabetical, based on days of the week or months of the year, we must create a custom sort order. Create a new spreadsheet workbook and enter the data shown in Table 5.7 in Sheet1.

Table 5.7

	A	B	C
1	**Student Number**	**Student Name**	**Grade**
2	1	Paul Thornton	Merit
3	2	Avril Green	Distinction
4	3	Mark Roberts	Fail
5	4	Cathy O Neill	Pass
6	5	Pauline Meehan	Merit
7	6	John Gallagher	Distinction
8	7	Bernard Tompkins	Merit
9	8	Yvonne O Donoghue	Merit
10	9	Tom Sheehan	Pass
11	10	Peter Ferns	Distinction

If we sort the grades in ascending alphabetical order, they will appear as distinction, fail, merit, pass or if we sort them in descending alphabetical order they will appear as pass, merit, fail, distinction. To sort the data so that it appears in order of distinction, merit, pass, fail or fail, pass, merit, distinction we must create a custom sort order.

1. Select **Tools** followed by **Options** from the menu.
2. Click the Custom Lists tab. In the Custom Lists box select NEW LIST and then click in the List Entries box.

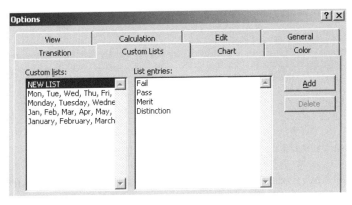

Figure 5.4

3. Type the new list as shown in Figure 5.4 and then click Add, followed by OK.
4. Click a cell in the Grade column (*any cell in the range C2:C11*).

5. Select **Data** followed by **Sort** from the menu and then select Grade from the 'Sort by' List.

6. Select Descending and then click Options.

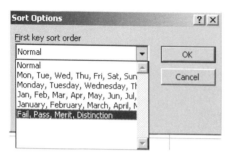

Figure 5.5

7. From the 'First key sort order' list select Fail, Pass, Merit, Distinction.

8. Click OK to close the Sort Options dialog box and then OK to implement the sort.

9. Save the spreadsheet as **Grades**.

Sorting Data by Columns Instead of Rows

Create a new spreadsheet workbook and enter the data shown in Table 5.8 in Sheet1.

Table 5.8

	A	B	C	D	E	F	G	H
1	Euro Conversion Rates							
2								
3	Country	USA	Japan	Britain	Canada	Norway	South Africa	Russia
4	Currency	Dollar	Yen	Pound	Dollar	Kroner	Rand	Rouble
5	Rate	0.883	115.85	0.613	1.397	7.638	9.918	27.554

1. Format all rates so that they display three places of decimals.

2. Highlight B3:H5.

3. Select **Data** followed by **Sort** from the menu and select Ascending as the 'Sort by' order.

4. Click Options. Under Orientation click 'Sort left to right' and then click OK twice.

5. Save the spreadsheet as **Exchange Rates**.

Tip: When sorting data by columns don't include the descriptions in the column to the left of the data that you're sorting.

Toolbar Buttons Introduced in Chapter Five

Figure 5.6 The **Sort Ascending** button

To sort a range of data in ascending order based on data in one column, select any cell in that column and then click the Sort Ascending button. For example, in a range of data containing a column of product descriptions and a column of prices, selecting any cell (except the heading) in the column of prices and then clicking the Sort Ascending button rearranges the entire list in ascending order of price.

Figure 5.7 The **Sort Descending** button

To sort a range of data in descending order based on data in one column, select any cell in that column and then click the Sort Descending button. For example, in a range of data containing a column of product descriptions and a column of prices, selecting any cell (except the heading) in the column of prices and then clicking the Sort Descending button rearranges the entire list in descending order of price.

Progress Test 1

Complete the test by writing answers in the space provided or by circling the correct answer.

1. A collection of worksheets is called a _____ .
2. A cell reference contained within a formula or function which remains constant when the formula or function is moved or copied is called a:

   a. relative cell reference
   b. absolute cell reference
   c. constant cell reference
   d. fixed cell reference.

3. In the spreadsheet displayed in Table 5.9 on Page 102, what formula is required to calculate a total of 684? _____

Table 5.9

	A	B
1	Price	120
2	Discount	5%
3	Quantity	6
4	Total	684

4. Assuming the name **sales** has been assigned to the range B2:G2 in the spreadsheet in Table 5.10 write down the functions required to calculate:

a. total units sold _____ .
b. average units sold _____ .
c. highest monthly sales _____ .
d. lowest monthly sales _____ .

Table 5.10

	A	B	C	D	E	F	G
1		Jan	Feb	Mar	Apr	May	Jun
2	Units	2084	3871	2593	2078	2688	3015

5. A useful method of making a cell reference absolute is to highlight the cell reference in a formula or function and press the _____ key.

6. Each set of numbers represented in a chart is called a

a. data range
b. data series
c. data base
d. data set.

7. Highlighting multiple ranges requires holding down the _____ key while dragging with the mouse.

8. Pressing the _____ key displays a list of cell and range names in a spreadsheet.

9. Which of the following charts can only display one data series?

a. column chart
b. bar chart
c. pie chart
d. XY chart.

10. Which of the following buttons will sort data in ascending order?

a.   b.

Figure 5.8   **Figure 5.9**

11. If the following list – Monday, Tuesday, Wednesday, Thursday, Friday – is sorted in ascending order, what will the resulting order be? _____

SECTION 2

Intermediate and Advanced Spreadsheet Assignments

Chapter 6: Spreadsheet Protection

- Restrict access to specific cells in a worksheet
- Prevent formulas and functions from being displayed in the formula bar
- Prevent users from deleting, renaming, moving, hiding or unhiding worksheets.

Chapter 7: IF Functions

- Create IF functions that make decisions based on single and multiple conditions
- Use conditional formatting to emphasise data.

Chapter 8: Lookup Functions

- Store data in a lookup table
- Use lookup functions to reference data stored in a lookup table.

Chapter 9: Pivot Tables

- Analyse data using a pivot table
- Create a pivot table report
- Create a pivot chart.

Chapter 10: Spreadsheet Macros

- Automate repetitive tasks with macros
- Run macros from shortcut keys and command buttons
- Update data using Paste Special
- Develop a custom menu system using macros and command buttons.

Progress Test 2

6

Spreadsheet Protection

In Chapter 6, you will learn how to

- Restrict access to specific cells in a worksheet
- Prevent formulas and functions from being displayed in the formula bar
- Prevent users from deleting, renaming, moving, hiding or unhiding worksheets.

Spreadsheet Protection

A spreadsheet workbook consists of a number of worksheets. Excel offers us two levels of protection for our spreadsheet workbooks:

1. Protecting the workbook prevents people from deleting, renaming, moving, hiding or unhiding worksheets contained within the workbook.
2. Protecting individual worksheets prevents people from deleting important data such as formulas, functions and headings stored in the worksheet.

In order to understand how spreadsheet protection works we will divide cells in a worksheet into four categories:

1. Cells where data is entered
2. Cells containing formulas/functions
3. Cells containing headings or numbers that rarely change
4. Cells that remain blank.

The example on page 108 is the spreadsheet named Rock Café, which was created in Chapter 2 in Table 6.1.

1. Data has been entered in the shaded cells
2. Formulas/functions have been entered in cells as displayed
3. Headings and numbers, which don't change, are displayed in cells with a heavy border
4. No data should be entered in the remaining empty cells.

Table 6.1

	A	B	C	D	E	F	G	H	I	J
1	Rock Café								Date	=today()
2										
3								Stalls	300	
4								Circle	350	
5								Balcony	250	
6										
7	Artist	Date	Stalls	%Full	Circle	%Full	Balcony	% Full	Total Tickets	%Full
8	The Corrs	08/09/2003	150	=C8/$I$3	300	=E8/$I$4	220	=G8/$I$5	=C8+E8+G8	=I8/sum($I$3:$I$5)
9	The Frames	10/09/2003	276	=C9/$I$3	245	=E9/$I$4	141	=G9/$I$5	=C9+E9+G9	=I9/sum($I$3:$I$5)
10	Aslan	11/09/2003	290	=C10/$I$3	307	=E10/$I$4	209	=G10/$I$5	=C10+E10+G10	=I10/sum($I$3:$I$5)
11	Jack L	14/09/2003	250	=C11/$I$3	312	=E11/$I$4	196	=G11/$I$5	=C11+E11+G11	=I11/sum($I$3:$I$5)
12	Westlife	18/09/2003	300	=C12/$I$3	350	=E12/$I$4	250	=G12/$I$5	=C12+E12+G12	=I12/sum($I$3:$I$5)
13	Ronan Keating	19/09/2003	100	=C13/$I$3	267	=E13/$I$4	233	=G13/$I$5	=C13+E13+G13	=I13/sum($I$3:$I$5)
14	Brian Kennedy	20/09/2003	180	=C14/$I$3	255	=E14/$I$4	200	=G14/$I$5	=C14+E14+G14	=I14/sum($I$3:$I$5)
15										
16	Total Sales		=sum(C8:C14)		=sum(E8:E14)		=sum(G8:G14)			
17	Average Sales		=average(C8:C14)		=average(E8:E14)		=average(G8:G14)			
18	Highest Sales		=max(C8:C14)		=max(E8:E14)		=max(G8:G14)			
19	Lowest Sales		=min(C8:C14)		=min(E8:E14)		=min(G8:G14)			
20	Number of Performances		=count(C8:C14)							

In this case, the objective of spreadsheet protection is to allow the spreadsheet user to enter data only in the shaded cells and to prevent the spreadsheet user from entering data in any other cells. Spreadsheet protection also allows us to hide formulas so that they don't appear in the formula bar.

Most students find spreadsheet protection confusing. The confusion arises out of the fact that instead of identifying cells to be protected, you identify cells where data entry is to be permitted. If you can remember this, the rest is relatively easy.

All cells in a worksheet are locked by default. Whether a cell is locked or unlocked doesn't actually have any effect until the worksheet is protected. *When the worksheet is protected, data can only be entered in cells that have been unlocked,* so it's very important to unlock cells that you want to have access to before protecting the worksheet. The spreadsheet user will be unable to enter data in locked cells once the worksheet is protected. Spreadsheet protection also allows us to hide formulas so that the spreadsheet user can't see them. In a business context, it's often the case that a spreadsheet is set up so that employees responsible for inputting data are unable to see how that data is processed, as this doesn't concern them.

What's important to remember is that protecting a worksheet without unlocking cells means that data can't be entered anywhere in that worksheet. It's not much good having a spreadsheet unless you can enter data in it!

Protecting the Worksheet

1. Highlight all cells where data will be entered (the shaded cells in Table 6.1). Select **Format** followed by **Cells** from the menu. Click the Protection tab. Remove the tick from the Locked checkbox to unlock these cells.

2. Highlight all cells containing formulas or functions. Select **Format** followed by **Cells** from the menu. Click the Protection tab. Click the Hidden checkbox to hide the formulas or functions contained in these cells. (**Note:** *Don't unlock the cells that you are hiding.*)

3. Select **Tools** followed by **Protection** and then **Protect Sheet** from the menu. Entering a password is advisable because it's easy for others to turn off spreadsheet protection if there is no password. Remember that passwords are case sensitive.

 Note: Steps one and two don't have any effect unless you carry out the third step. Once you've carried out step three, you will only be able to enter data in cells that have been unlocked. Formulas will not be displayed in the formula bar.

Protecting Worksheets – Additional Points

When you select Tools, Protection then Protect Sheet you will see the dialog box in Figure 6.1 on page 110.

Figure 6.1

Contents

Clicking this box has the following effects.

- Users will only be able to enter data in cells that were unlocked before protecting the worksheet
- Formulas that were hidden before the worksheet was protected won't be displayed in the formula bar
- Rows or columns that were hidden before the worksheet was protected can't be unhidden.

Objects

If you click this box, users will be unable to make changes to graphic objects such as charts, maps, clip art and pictures.

Scenarios

A scenario is a type of spreadsheet model and is not covered in this book. If you click this box, users will be unable to view scenarios or make changes to scenarios.

Protecting the Workbook

Protecting the workbook is more straightforward. Simply select **Tools** followed by **Protection** and then **Protect Workbook** from the menu. This prevents others from deleting, renaming, moving, hiding or unhiding worksheets contained in the workbook.

It's advisable to protect the workbook together with individual worksheets contained within the workbook. This is because protecting a worksheet without protecting the workbook means that the entire worksheet can be deleted, regardless of the fact that access to certain cells within the worksheet has been restricted.

Protecting Workbooks – Additional Points

When you select Tools, Protection then Protect Workbook you will see the dialog box in Figure 6.2.

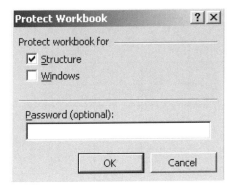

Figure 6.2

Structure

Clicking this box prevents users from:

- Viewing worksheets that you have hidden
- Moving, deleting, hiding or renaming worksheets
- Inserting new worksheets or chart sheets
- Moving or copying worksheets to another workbook
- Recording new macros.

Windows

Clicking this box prevents users from:

- Changing the size or position of windows within the workbook
- Moving, resizing or closing workbook windows.

 Spreadsheet Protection Assignment One

1. Open the spreadsheet named Rock Café (created in Chapter 2: Spreadsheet Functions).
2. Rename Sheet1 as Ticket Sales.
3. Implement spreadsheet protection so that data can only be entered in the ranges A8:C14, E8:E14 and G8:G14 and so that formulas and functions are not displayed in the formula bar.

 Tip: When unlocking cells or hiding formulas, multiple ranges can be selected by holding down the CTRL key.

4. Delete all unused worksheets and protect the workbook for structure and windows.

5. Erase data from unlocked cells and enter new data displayed in bold print in Table 6.2. (**Note:** *At this point you shouldn't be able to delete formulas, functions or headings.*)

Table 6.2

	A	B	C	D	E	F	G	H	I	J
1	Rock Café								Date	
2										
3								Stalls	300	
4								Circle	350	
5								Balcony	250	
6										
7	Artist	Date	Stalls	%Full	Circle	%Full	Balcony	% Full	Total Tickets	%Full
8	Coldplay	03/10/2003	288		306		244			
9	Stereophonics	05/10/2003	275		323		239			
10	Sheryl Crow	06/10/2003	280		344		231			
11	Alanis Morissette	08/10/2003	298		350		247			
12	Juliet Turner	09/10/2003	249		298		132			
13	David Gray	10/10/2003	300		350		250			
14	Van Morrison	12/10/2003	280		325		250			

Tip: Pressing the TAB key moves the cell pointer between unlocked cells in a protected worksheet.

6. Check the Sales Chart to see that it reflects the new data.
7. Click the Save button to save the changes.

Tip: If you need to increase the width of a column so that new data is displayed fully, you will have to unprotect the worksheet, adjust column width and then re-protect the worksheet.

Spreadsheet Protection Assignment Two

1. Open the spreadsheet named Ticket Sales Galway-Dublin Route (created in Chapter 3: Naming and Linking Worksheets).
2. Implement spreadsheet protection so that data can only be entered in cell A1 and in the range B5:H9 in the 0745, 1100 and 1510 worksheets. No data entry is permitted in the worksheet named Weekly Ticket Sales.
3. Formulas shouldn't be displayed in the formula bar of any worksheet.

4. Delete all unused worksheets and protect the workbook for structure and windows.

5. Erase data from unlocked cells in the 0745, 1100 and 1510 sheets. (***Note:*** *At this point you shouldn't be able to delete formulas, functions or headings.*)

6. Enter the data displayed in bold print in Table 6.3 in the worksheet named 0745.

Table 6.3

	A	B	C	D	E	F	G	H
1	**Week 2 Ticket Sales**							
2	Galway-Dublin departing 07:45							
3								
4		Galway	Athenry	Ballinasloe	Athlone	Tullamore	Portarlington	Kildare
5	Monday	**241**	**40**	**61**	**100**	**89**	**76**	**172**
6	Tuesday	**168**	**25**	**42**	**89**	**90**	**54**	**145**
7	Wednesday	**145**	**20**	**38**	**70**	**87**	**53**	**140**
8	Thursday	**159**	**23**	**39**	**75**	**82**	**49**	**155**
9	Friday	**221**	**25**	**45**	**88**	**106**	**82**	**195**

7. Enter the data displayed in bold print in Table 6.4 in the worksheet named 1100.

Table 6.4

	A	B	C	D	E	F	G	H
1	**Week 2 Ticket Sales**							
2	Galway-Dublin departing 11:00							
3								
4		Galway	Athenry	Ballinasloe	Athlone	Tullamore	Portarlington	Kildare
5	Monday	**61**	**12**	**24**	**37**	**21**	**25**	**44**
6	Tuesday	**45**	**5**	**19**	**25**	**31**	**12**	**36**
7	Wednesday	**31**	**2**	**10**	**32**	**26**	**14**	**23**
8	Thursday	**34**	**1**	**10**	**23**	**33**	**17**	**29**
9	Friday	**76**	**6**	**22**	**28**	**31**	**21**	**38**

8. Enter the data displayed in bold print in Table 6.5 in the worksheet named 1510.

Table 6.5

	A	B	C	D	E	F	G	H
1	Week 2 Ticket Sales							
2	Galway-Dublin departing 15:10							
3								
4		Galway	Athenry	Ballinasloe	Athlone	Tullamore	Portarlington	Kildare
5	Monday	47	12	14	23	24	28	45
6	Tuesday	39	6	1	12	25	21	36
7	Wednesday	30	8	4	8	10	19	42
8	Thursday	22	8	8	13	19	23	44
9	Friday	36	12	20	31	36	29	60

9. Unprotect the workbook and create a column chart that displays data in the range A4:H9 from the Weekly Ticket Sales worksheet with station names on the horizontal axis and daily sales represented by columns. The chart title is Weekly Ticket Sales by Station. The title for the y axis is Tickets Sold. Display the chart on a separate chart sheet named Sales Chart.

10. Re-protect the workbook and click the Save button to save the changes.

Tip: When you're hiding the contents of cells that contain formulas or functions, make sure that you don't unlock these cells. Unlocking them would mean that the formulas or functions could be deleted.

7

IF Functions

In Chapter 7, you will learn how to

- Create IF functions that make decisions based on single and multiple conditions
- Use conditional formatting to emphasise data.

An IF function is a special type of function that can make a decision based on information supplied to it by the spreadsheet user. We will learn about IF functions by designing a spreadsheet for the Online Insurance Company. The spreadsheet will contain IF functions that will make a number of decisions as part of the process of calculating the premium for each Online Insurance customer. Because Online Insurance deals with hundreds of customers every day, the spreadsheet will greatly reduce the workload of its sales representatives by automating decision-making with IF functions.

Online Insurance specialise in motor insurance. They charge a basic premium of €300 and then add to this amount as follows.

Gender premium: Male drivers are charged 20% extra on the basic premium.

Age premium:

- For drivers aged 18 or under, there is an extra charge of 60% of the basic premium
- For drivers aged between 19 and 21 inclusive, there is an extra charge of 40% of the basic premium
- For drivers aged between 22 and 25 inclusive, there is an extra charge of 20% of the basic premium
- For drivers older than 25, there is an extra charge of 10% of the basic premium.

Performance premium: Drivers with sports cars that have an engine capacity above 1600cc are charged 40% extra on the basic premium.

Claims bonus: Drivers who are either over 30 or who have no previous claims are entitled to a reduction of 5% of the basic premium.

Licence bonus:

- Full licence holders aged 18 or under get a reduction of 1% off the basic premium
- Full licence holders aged between 19 and 21 inclusive get a reduction of 2% off the basic premium

- Full licence holders aged between 22 and 25 inclusive get a reduction of 3% off the basic premium
- Full licence holders aged between 26 and 70 inclusive get a reduction of 5% off the basic premium
- No reduction is given to drivers who don't hold a full licence or to drivers aged 71 or older.

From the above information it can be seen that the total premium for each customer depends on five factors: gender, age, performance of the car, previous claims and licence. It would be very difficult for the sales representatives to calculate premiums manually because each quotation would require five separate decisions. In order to make each decision the sales representative would have to refer to documentation detailing rules and premiums and, having calculated the individual premiums, would then have to calculate the total premium. This process would be very slow and with so many customers, errors would inevitably be made. Newer staff would take considerably longer to calculate the total premium until they were trained in properly.

As you work through this chapter you will learn how to create a spreadsheet to automate each of these decisions using IF functions.

Each additional premium or bonus requires a separate IF function to make the decision. We will see that there are four different types of IF functions. These are as follows:

1. Simple IF function
2. Nested simple IF function
3. Compound IF function
4. Nested compound IF function.

When you have completed the chapter, the Online Insurance spreadsheet will calculate the total premium based on data entered relating to each of the five factors already mentioned. The task of decision-making will be taken over by the spreadsheet, allowing the sales representatives to provide quick and accurate quotations. They won't have to refer to the rules governing the premiums since these rules will be stored in the IF functions themselves.

Structure of an IF Function

Each IF function consists of a condition, a true action and a false action. Later on in this chapter we will see that more complex IF functions can have more than one condition and more than two actions.

Condition

This is where the IF function carries out some kind of test, using a logical operator. The following logical operators, as shown in Table 7.1, can be used in a condition.

Table 7.1

Logical Operator	Meaning
=	Equal to
<	Less than
<=	Less than or equal to
>	Greater than
>=	Greater than or equal to
<>	Not equal to

Logical operators are combined with cell references, values and text to form logical expressions. Examples of logical expressions are shown below in Table 7.2.

Table 7.2

Logical Expression	Meaning
A2>10	Check if the value in A2 is greater than 10
B12<>"Monday"	Check if the text in B12 is not equal to Monday
D5=E5	Check if the text or value in D5 is equal to the text or value in E5
sum(C2:C6)<=100	Check if the sum of the numbers in the range C2:C6 is less than or equal to 100

True Action

The true action is implemented when the condition is satisfied. The true action may be a formula, or a number or text. Examples of true actions are shown below in Table 7.3.

Table 7.3

True Action	Meaning
C5*5%	Multiply the value in C5 by 5% and enter the result in the current cell
100	Enter the value 100 in the current cell
"Pass"	Enter the text Pass in the current cell

False Action

The false action is implemented when the condition is not satisfied. Just like the true action, the false action may be a formula, a number or text.

Simple IF Function

A simple IF function is required where the IF function must decide to take one of two possible courses of action. The decision is based on a single condition. When the condition is satisfied the first course of action is taken. The second course of action is taken when the condition is not satisfied. A simple IF function has three sections: the condition, the true action and the false action.

Calculating the Gender Premium

A Simple IF function will be used to calculate the gender premium for the Online Insurance Company. For male drivers there is an extra charge of 20% of the basic premium.

- Condition   : is the driver male?
- True action   : male drivers are charged 20% extra
- False action : drivers who aren't male aren't charged extra.

Structure of the Simple IF Function

= if(condition, true action, false action)

Table 7.4

	A	B	C	D	E
1				Basic Premium	€300
2				Total Premium	
3	Policy Holder	Jim Collins			
4	Gender	Male	Gender Premium	= if(B4 ="Male",E1*20%,0)	
5	Age	27			
6	Full Drivers Licence	Yes	then		otherwise
7	Engine cc	1800			
8	Sports Model	Yes			
9	Claims to Date	0			

Writing the IF Function

In the spreadsheet displayed in Table 7.4, the task of the IF function is to check if the text "Male" was entered in B4. The condition and resulting action are summarised in Table 7.5.

Table 7.5

Condition	Resulting Action
Gender	Gender Premium
"Male"	20% of basic premium

If 'Male' wasn't entered in B4 then the gender premium is zero. The IF function is entered in D4 as shown in Table 7.5.

Points to Note

1. The condition and the true action are followed by commas. The first comma represents the word 'then' and the second comma represents the word 'otherwise'. If we were to write the IF function in English, we would get the following: 'If B4 is equal to male then multiply E1 by 20%, otherwise enter zero in D4.' In this case because B4 is equal to male, then E1 is multiplied by 20%, giving 60, and this number is displayed in D4.

2. When an IF function is testing for text (here we are testing to see if B4 contains the text 'Male'), the text must be enclosed in inverted commas.

IF Functions Rule One: When testing for text in an IF function, the text should be enclosed in inverted commas. This rule applies to all types of IF functions.

Simple IF Assignment One

Create a new spreadsheet workbook and enter the data shown in Table 7.6 on page 120. Enter formulas and functions in the shaded cells to complete the spreadsheet.

1. Calculate the total for each product.
2. Create a simple IF function to calculate the discount. There is a discount of 10% of the total where the total is greater than 300. There is no discount where the total is 300 or less.
3. Calculate the discounted price.
4. Format all money amounts to currency.
5. Sort the data in descending order of discounted price.
6. Save the spreadsheet as **Discount Calculations**.

Table 7.6

	A	B	C	D	E	F
1	Product	Unit Price	Quantity	Total	Discount	Discounted Price
2	Card Index Cabinet	47.23	3			
3	Fortress Cash Box	20.41	1			
4	Junior Manual Typist Chair	219.94	10			
5	Computer Stand	14.7	10			
6	Keyboard Desk	136.8	5			
7	PC Desk	143.64	2			
8	Mobile Work Station	214.8	3			
9	Extension Shelves	27.43	2			
10	Low Level Printer Stand	76.62	4			
11	General Purpose Trolley	162	1			

 ## Conditional Formatting

Conditional formatting is a useful way of emphasising certain information contained in a spreadsheet by applying a particular format to that information. For example, in the Discount Calculations spreadsheet we could use conditional formatting to emphasise the discount amounts in red, bold italics. Conditional formatting is implemented in two distinct steps.

1. Identify the cells that you want to apply formatting to. For discount amounts this is all values in the range E2:E11 that are greater than zero.
2. Specify a way of formatting the cells identified in step one above. For example, we could format all discount amounts with a font colour of red and with a style of bold italic.

Using Conditional Formatting – Worked Example

1. Open the Discount Calculations spreadsheet.
2. Highlight the range containing discount amounts (E2:E11).
3. Select **Format** followed by **Conditional Formatting** from the menu.
4. In the Conditional Formatting dialog box, shown in Figure 7.1, we must firstly identify the cells that we want to format (the discount amounts) in the highlighted range. What distinguishes the discount amounts from other values in this range is that they are greater than zero.

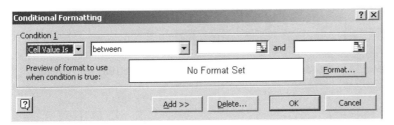

Figure 7.1

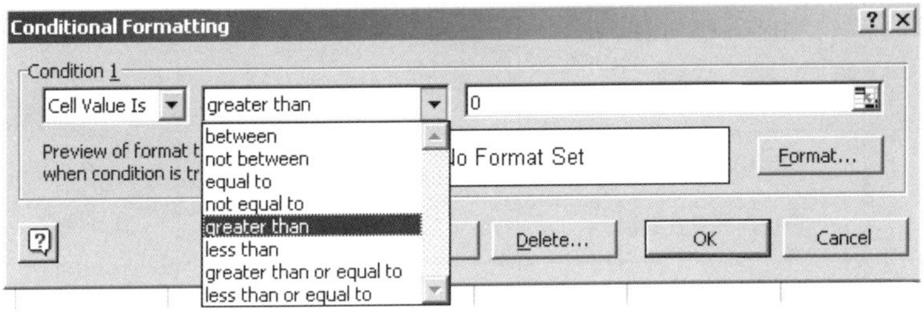

Figure 7.2

5. Select 'greater than' and type 0, as shown in Figure 7.2.

6. Having identified the cells that we want to format, we must now define how we want those cells to be formatted by creating a Format Set. In the Conditional Formatting dialog box, click the Format button and select Bold Italic as the font style and red as the font colour.

7. Click OK twice to apply the formatting. Discount amounts are emphasised in red, bold italics.

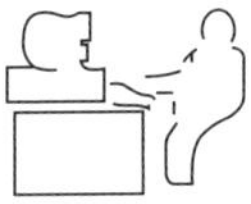

Simple IF Assignment Two

Create a new spreadsheet workbook and enter the data shown in Table 7.7 on page 122. Enter functions in the shaded cells to complete the spreadsheet.

1. Create a simple IF function to display the text 'Pass' or 'Fail'. The pass mark is 60%.

2. Sort the data in descending order of marks out of 100.

3. Use conditional formatting to emphasise the marks out of 100 of students who failed in red, bold italics.

4. Rename Sheet1 as Exam Data.

5. Delete all unused worksheets.

6. Implement spreadsheet protection so that data can only be entered in the range A2:C12 and so that formulas and functions aren't displayed in the formula bar. Protect the workbook for structure and windows.

7. Print the Exam Data worksheet with gridlines and row and column headings displayed.

8. Save the spreadsheet as **Results**.

Table 7.7

	A	B	C	D
1	Exam Number	Student Name	Marks out of 100	Result
2	990101	Mark O Neill	46	
3	990102	Tony Meehan	70	
4	990103	Jane Smith	58	
5	990104	Eileen O Sullivan	61	
6	990105	Pete Greene	83	
7	990106	Paula Jones	31	
8	990107	Evelyn Andrews	58	
9	990108	Aidan Jackson	76	
10	990109	Mike Jennings	60	
11	990110	Tanya Ryan	59	
12	990111	Richard Byrne	90	

Tip: To delete multiple worksheets, hold down the CTRL key and click the worksheet tab of each worksheet you want to delete. Once you have selected all the worksheets you want to delete, right click any selected worksheet and select Delete from the menu. Click OK to confirm that you want to delete the selected worksheets.

Simple IF Assignment Three

The spreadsheet displayed in Table 7.8 calculates the climb or descent, in metres, as hill walkers go from one location to the next. Create a new spreadsheet workbook and enter the data shown in Table 7.8. Enter functions in the shaded cells to complete the spreadsheet.

1. Calculate climb (metres) using an IF function. (**Hint:** When the height of the current location is greater than the height of the previous location, the climb is calculated by subtracting the height of the previous location from the height of the current location.)

2. Calculate descent (metres) using a similar IF function.

3. Use conditional formatting to emphasise climbs above 150 metres in red, bold italics.

4. Use conditional formatting to emphasise all descents in blue, bold italics.

5. Rename Sheet1 as Walk Plan.

6. Delete all unused worksheets.

Table 7.8

	A	B	C	D	E
1	Location No	Name of Area	Height (metres)	Climb (metres)	Descent (metres)
2	1	Drumgoff Bridge	120	-	
3	2	Carraway Stick Mountain	597		
4	3	Corrigasleggaun	794		
5	4	Lugnaquilla	925		
6	5	Cannow Mountain	712		
7	6	Camenabologue	758		
8	7	Table Mountain	701		
9	8	Conavalla	734		
10	9	Lugduff	652		
11	10	Mullacor	657		

7. Display the data using a stacked column chart where mountain heights, climb (metres) and descent (metres) are represented by column sections. The chart title is Peaks, Climbs and Descents. The title for the y axis is Height (metres). Click the Data Labels tab and select the Show Values option to display the value represented by each column section. The chart should be on a separate chart sheet named Climb Profile.

8. Implement spreadsheet protection so that data can only be entered in the range A2:C11 and so that formulas and functions aren't displayed in the formula bar. Protect the workbook for structure and windows.

9. Save the spreadsheet as **Hillwalk**.

 Tip: If Excel displays the text False as the result of an IF function, it means that you have left out the false action.

 Simple IF Assignment Four

Create a new spreadsheet workbook and enter the data shown in Table 7.9 on page 124. Enter formulas and functions in the shaded cells to complete the spreadsheet. (**Note**: *There is no need to wrap text, as displayed.*)

1. Calculate annual TFA (tax free allowance) using an IF function. This is €4000 for married people and €2000 for single people.

2. Calculate weekly pay, weekly TFA and weekly taxable pay.

Table 7.9

	A	B	C	D	E	F	G	H	I
1	Employee Name	Annual Salary	Marital Status	Annual TFA	Weekly Pay	Weekly TFA	Weekly Taxable Pay	Weekly Tax	Net Pay
2	Paul Sheehan	18900	Single						
3	Mike Everett	21550	Married						
4	Tina Lovett	14720	Single						
5	Barry Walsh	29880	Single						
6	Karl Burke	12940	Married						
7	Andrea Livingston	31000	Married						
8	Cathy Dunne	22440	Single						
9	Adrian Looney	15000	Single						
10	Liam Nocton	20300	Married						
11	Niall Donnelly	22000	Married						

3. Calculate the weekly tax using an IF function. Employees who earn up to €300 inclusive pay tax of 25% on their weekly taxable pay. Employees who earn more than €300 pay tax at 25% on the first €300 of their weekly taxable pay and are taxed at 40% on the amount above €300.

4. Calculate net pay.

5. Format all money amounts to currency.

6. Use conditional formatting to emphasise all weekly tax amounts that are greater than 100 in red, bold italics.

7. Format the data using Autoformat, Classic 2 (Autoformat is a quick way to format your data. Highlight from A1 to I11. Select **Format** followed by **Autoformat** from the menu. Select Classic 2 and then click OK).

8. Sort the data first in descending order of marital status and then in descending order of weekly pay.

9. Rename Sheet1 as Employee Payroll. Delete all unused worksheets in the workbook.

10. Save the spreadsheet as **Employee Payroll**.

Tip: Never use the €sign in a formula or function as this will result in a number being interpreted as text and return an error.

Advanced Conditional Formatting

We have already seen how conditional formatting can be used to emphasise certain text or values within a particular range. First we highlight a range of cells and then isolate particular cell values within that range using the Conditional Formatting dialog box.

Figure 7.3

In the example above from the Employee Payroll spreadsheet, all weekly tax amounts in the highlighted range that are greater than 100 are formatted in red, bold italics. The formatting is dependent on a value entered by the spreadsheet user in the Conditional Formatting dialog box, as shown above.

Advanced conditional formatting is where formatting is dependant on values stored in other cells in the worksheet outside the highlighted area. A formula is used to refer to these cells. In the Employee Payroll spreadsheet, advanced conditional formatting can be used to emphasise the names of employees whose weekly tax is greater than €100 in red, bold italics.

Using Advanced Formatting – Worked Example

1. Open the Employee Payroll spreadsheet.
2. Highlight the employee names (A2:A11).
3. Select Format followed by Conditional Formatting from the menu.

The format of cells in the range A2:A11 is dependant on values entered in the range H2:H11 (whether an employee name is displayed in red, bold italics depends on the weekly tax that employee pays. The weekly tax amounts are stored in the range H2:H11).

4. Under Condition 1 select Formula Is.
5. Type the formula displayed in Figure 7.4 and select red, bold italics as the Format Set.

Figure 7.4

6. Click OK twice to apply the formatting.

The names of employees whose weekly tax is above €100 are displayed in red, bold italics.

Simple IF Assignment Five

Create a new spreadsheet workbook and enter the data shown in Table 7.10.

Table 7.10

	A	B
	Employee No	**Employee Name**
1		
2	1	Paul Sheehan
3	2	Mike Everett
4	3	Tina Lovett
5	4	Barry Walsh
6	5	Karl Burke
7	6	Andrea Livingston
8	7	Cathy Dunne
9	8	Adrian Looney
10	9	Liam Nocton
11	10	Niall Donnelly

1. Rename Sheet1 as Employee List.
2. Implement spreadsheet protection so that data cannot be entered in this worksheet.
3. Rename Sheet2 as Monday.
4. Enter the data displayed in Table 7.11 in the worksheet named Monday. Formulas and functions will be entered in the shaded cells.

Table 7.11

	A	B	C	D	E
1	Monday Timesheet				
2					
3	Employee No	Employee Name	Clock-In Time	Due In At	Status
4			08:57	09:00	
5			09:50	10:00	
6			11:15	11:00	
7			09:03	09:00	
8			08:32	09:00	
9			09:47	10:00	
10			10:30	10:00	
11			09:21	09:00	
12			08:50	09:00	
13			08:56	10:00	

 Tip: Hours and minutes must be separated by a colon in order for Excel to interpret the value entered in the cell as time. Using a decimal point instead of a colon will cause Excel to interpret the value as a number.

5. Use linking formulas to read the employee numbers and employee names from the Employee List worksheet. (**Note**: *Refer to Chapter 3 for an explanation of linking formulas.*)

6. Use IF functions to display the status of each employee, which is either late or on time.

7. Use conditional formatting to emphasise both the names of employees who were late and their status in red, bold italics.

8. Implement spreadsheet protection so that data can only be entered in A1 and in the range C4:C13 and so that formulas and functions aren't displayed in the formula bar.

9. Copy the worksheet named Monday and rename the copy as Tuesday. (**Note**: *The copy will initially be named Monday(2).*)

10. In the worksheet named Tuesday, change the title to Tuesday Timesheet, delete the existing clock-in times and enter the new times shown in bold print in Table 7.12 on page 128.

11. Copy the worksheet named Tuesday and rename the copy as Wednesday.

12. In the worksheet named Wednesday, change the title to Wednesday Timesheet, delete the existing clock-in times and enter the new times shown in bold print in Table 7.13 on page 128.

Table 7.12

	A	B	C	D	E
1	Tuesday Timesheet				
2					
3	Employee No	Employee Name	Clock-In Time	Due In At	Status
4			08:50	09:00	
5			09:59	10:00	
6			11:01	11:00	
7			08:50	09:00	
8			08:30	09:00	
9			09:53	10:00	
10			09:50	10:00	
11			09:03	09:00	
12			08:33	09:00	
13			08:41	10:00	

Table 7.13

	A	B	C	D	E
1	Wednesday Timesheet				
2					
3	Employee No	Employee Name	Clock-In Time	Due In At	Status
4			08:50	09:00	
5			09:56	10:00	
6			11:07	11:00	
7			08:49	09:00	
8			08:40	09:00	
9			09:58	10:00	
10			10:30	10:00	
11			08:57	09:00	
12			09:00	09:00	
13			08:55	10:00	

13. Copy the worksheet named Wednesday and rename the copy as Thursday.

14. In the worksheet named Thursday, change the title to Thursday Timesheet, delete the existing clock-in times and enter the new times shown in bold print in Table 7.14.

Table 7.14

	A	B	C	D	E
1	Thursday Timesheet				
2					
3	Employee No	Employee Name	Clock-In Time	Due In At	Status
4			08:58	09:00	
5			09:23	10:00	
6			11:45	11:00	
7			08:50	09:00	
8			08:53	09:00	
9			09:55	10:00	
10			09:21	10:00	
11			08:59	09:00	
12			08:57	09:00	
13			08:56	10:00	

15. Copy the worksheet named Thursday and rename the copy as Friday.

16. In the worksheet named Friday, change the title to Friday Timesheet, delete the existing clock-in times and enter the new times shown in bold print in Table 7.15 on page 130.

17. Enter the data in Table 7.16 on page 130 in an unused worksheet within the same workbook, or insert a new worksheet if necessary. Formulas and functions will be entered in the shaded cells.

18. Use linking formulas to read the employee names from the Employee List worksheet.

19. In columns B, C, D, E and F use a linking formula to read the daily status of each employee.

20. Use the COUNTIF function to calculate the number of lates for each employee.

21. Use conditional formatting to emphasise the names of all employees who were late and the number of times they were late in red, bold italics.

22. Rename this worksheet as Summary.

23. Implement spreadsheet protection so that data cannot be entered in this worksheet and so that all formulas are hidden.

24. Delete all unused worksheets in the workbook.

Table 7.15

	A	B	C	D	E
1	Friday Timesheet				
2					
3	Employee No	Employee Name	Clock-In Time	Due In At	Status
4			08:48	09:00	
5			09:45	10:00	
6			11:01	11:00	
7			08:45	09:00	
8			08:55	09:00	
9			09:44	10:00	
10			09:55	10:00	
11			09:00	09:00	
12			09:03	09:00	
13			09:01	10:00	

Table 7.16

	A	B	C	D	E	F	G
1	Weekly Attendance Summary						
2							
3	Employee Name	Monday	Tuesday	Wednesday	Thursday	Friday	Number of Lates
4							
5							
6							
7							
8							
9							
10							
11							
12							
13							

25. If necessary, rearrange worksheets so that they appear in the order displayed in Figure 7.5.

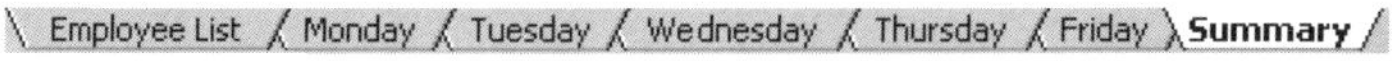

\ Employee List ⟋ Monday ⟋ Tuesday ⟋ Wednesday ⟋ Thursday ⟋ Friday ⟍**Summary** ⟋

Figure 7.5

26. Protect the workbook for structure and windows.
27. Save the spreadsheet as **Employee Timesheet**.

 ## Nested Simple IF Function

A nested simple IF function is required where the IF function must decide to take one of three or more possible courses of action. Each decision is based on a single condition. The course of action taken is the one for which the condition is satisfied.

The simple IF function only allows us to have two possible courses of action: a true action and a false action. Where there are three or more possible courses of action we must start a second IF function inside the first IF function. This is why it's called a nested simple IF function.

 Note: The word 'simple' indicates that each action depends on only one condition.

Calculating the Age Premium

Returning to our Online Insurance Company spreadsheet we'll see how a nested simple IF function is used to calculate the age premium.

Age premium:

• For drivers aged 18 or under there's an extra charge of 60% of the basic premium
• For drivers aged between 19 and 21 inclusive there's an extra charge of 40% of the basic premium
• For drivers aged between 22 and 25 inclusive there's an extra charge of 20% of the basic premium
• For drivers older than 25 there's an extra charge of 10% of the basic premium.

In a nested simple IF function there are three or more possible courses of action. In this case there are four possible courses of action. An additional premium of 60%, 40%, 20% or 10% could be charged, depending on the age of the driver. A condition is required for each of the first three possible courses of action. The fourth course of action is taken if none of the first three conditions are satisfied.

Four conditions: is the driver 18 or under, is the driver 19–21, is the driver 22–25 or is the driver over 25?

Four actions: 60% for 18 or under, 40% for 19–21, 20% for 22–25 and 10% for over 25.

Structure of the Nested Simple IF Function

= if(condition1, action1, if (condition2, action2, if(condition3, action3, action4)))

 Note: The number of conditions in a nested simple IF function will vary according to the number of possible courses of action. Excel allows a maximum of seven IFs nested inside the first IF.

Table 7.17

	A	B	C	D	E	F
1				Basic Premium	€ 300	
2				Total Premium		
3	Policy Holder	Jim Collins				
4	Gender	Male	Gender Premium	€ 60		
5	Age	27	Age Premium	=if(B5<=18,E1*60%,if(B5<=21,E1*40%, if(B5<=25,E1*20%,E1*10%)))		
6	Full Drivers Licence	Yes				
7	Engine cc	1800				
8	Sports Model	Yes				
9	Claims to Date	0				

Writing the IF Function

In the spreadsheet displayed in Table 7.17, the task of the IF function is to check the age that was entered in B5. The conditions and resulting actions are summarised in Table 7.18.

Table 7.18

	Condition	Resulting Action
	Age	Age Premium
1	<=18	60% of basic premium
2	19–21 inclusive	40% of basic premium
3	22–25 inclusive	20% of basic premium
4	>25	10% of basic premium

In this case, the age in B5 is greater than 25 so the age premium is calculated by multiplying E1 by 10%, giving 30. The IF function is entered in D5 as shown in Table 7.17 on page 132.

Points to Note

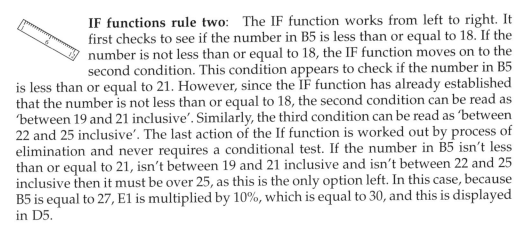

IF functions rule two: The IF function works from left to right. It first checks to see if the number in B5 is less than or equal to 18. If the number is not less than or equal to 18, the IF function moves on to the second condition. This condition appears to check if the number in B5 is less than or equal to 21. However, since the IF function has already established that the number is not less than or equal to 18, the second condition can be read as 'between 19 and 21 inclusive'. Similarly, the third condition can be read as 'between 22 and 25 inclusive'. The last action of the If function is worked out by process of elimination and never requires a conditional test. If the number in B5 isn't less than or equal to 21, isn't between 19 and 21 inclusive and isn't between 22 and 25 inclusive then it must be over 25, as this is the only option left. In this case, because B5 is equal to 27, E1 is multiplied by 10%, which is equal to 30, and this is displayed in D5.

IF functions rule three: The number of IFs is always one less than the number of actions, e.g. three actions means two IFs are required, four actions means three IFs are required, five actions means four IFs are required, and so on.

IF functions rule four: The last action never requires a condition test.

IF functions rule five: When testing for numbers in different ranges, either start at the highest number and work downwards or start at the lowest number and work upwards.

IF functions rule six: When testing for numbers in different ranges in a nested IF function, all the signs should be pointing in the same direction, e.g. all greater than (>) signs or all less than (<) signs.

IF functions rule seven: The number of IFs determines how many brackets should be closed at the end of a nested simple IF function, e.g. two IFs means two brackets should be closed, three IFs means three brackets should be closed, four IFs means four brackets should be closed, and so on.

Nested Simple IF Assignment One

Create a new spreadsheet workbook and enter the data shown in Table 7.19. Enter formulas and functions in the shaded cells to complete the spreadsheet.

Table 7.19

	A	B	C	D	E	F	G
1	Customer Name	Model Name	Days Hired	Cost per Day	Total	Discount	Amount Due
2	Frank Dunne	Fiesta	2	45			
3	Oliver O Shea	Mondeo	6	55			
4	Pat Murphy	Ka	1	35			
5	Michael O Neill	Focus	8	50			
6	Michelle Murray	Clio	14	40			
7	Alex Evans	Megane	5	50			
8	Kevin Fanning	Corolla	14	50			
9	Ciaran Molloy	Sunny	14	50			

1. Calculate the total.
2. Calculate the discount using an IF function. There is no discount on cars hired for five days or less. There is a discount of 5% of the total on cars hired for six to ten days. There is a discount of 10% of the total on cars hired for more than ten days.
3. Calculate the amount due.
4. Format all money amounts to currency.
5. Sort the data in descending order of amount due.
6. Format the data using Autoformat, Classic 1.
7. Rename Sheet1 as Customer Records.
8. Delete all unused worksheets in the workbook.
9. Implement spreadsheet protection so that data can only be entered in the range A2:D9 and so that formulas and functions aren't displayed in the formula bar. Protect the workbook for structure and windows.
10. Print the Customer Records worksheet.
11. Save the spreadsheet as **Car Hire**.

Tip: If you're having difficulty with an IF function, break it down into sections. Work out each action using a separate formula.

Nested Simple IF Assignment Two

Create a new spreadsheet workbook and enter the data shown in Table 7.20. Enter formulas and functions in the shaded cells to complete the spreadsheet.

Table 7.20

	A	B	C	D	E
1	**Job Description**	**Status**	**Basic Price**	**Additional Charge**	**Total**
2	Deliver goods to Clondalkin	Urgent	45		
3	Pick up package in Swords	Normal	35		
4	Collect documents at Four Courts	Normal	30		
5	Deliver package to Dun Laoghaire	Priority	45		
6	Pick up computers at airport	Urgent	50		
7	Deliver stationary to Blackrock	Normal	35		
8	Collect faulty PC at Sandyford	Urgent	40		
9	Courier airline ticket to Bray	Urgent	60		
10	Deliver exam papers to Athlone	Priority	150		
11	Deliver important documents to Sandymount	Urgent	30		

1. Calculate the additional charge using an IF function as follows. There is no additional charge for deliveries whose status is normal. There is an additional charge of 20% of the basic price for deliveries whose status is urgent. There is an additional charge of 50% of the basic price for deliveries whose status is priority.

2. Calculate the total.

3. Format all money amounts to currency.

4. Use conditional formatting to display the status of priority deliveries in red, bold italics.

5. Rename Sheet1 as Delivery List. Delete all unused worksheets in the workbook.

6. Implement spreadsheet protection so that data can only be entered in the range A2:C11 and so that formulas and functions aren't displayed in the formula bar. Protect the workbook for structure and windows.

7. Save the spreadsheet as **Delivery Charges**.

Nested Simple IF Assignment Three

Create a new spreadsheet workbook and enter the data shown in Table 7.21 on page 136. Enter formulas and functions in the shaded cells to complete the spreadsheet.

Tip: The Merge and Center button shown in Figure 7.6 can be used to centre a heading within a range of selected cells. Enter the main heading in A1. Highlight A1:I1 and then click the Merge and Center button. Repeat these steps to centre the sub-heading.

Table 7.21

	A	B	C	D	E	F	G	H	I
1	DON'T RISKIT INSURANCE								
2	Household Policies								
3									
4	Client Name	House Value	Contents Value	Payment Option	House Premium	Contents Premium	Total Premium	Initial Payment	Monthly Instalment
5	Joe Murphy	265000	8500	B					
6	Mary Horgan	280000	11250	B					
7	Peter Lynch	325000	25000	A					
8	Dave Power	278000	15000	C					
9	Margaret O'Neill	220000	13500	B					
10	Paul Hewitt	500000	17000	A					
11	Colin O'Sullivan	215000	7000	C					
12	Eddy Jones	450000	25000	A					
13	Gerry Thompson	475000	8500	C					

Merge and Center button

Figure 7.6

1. Calculate the house premium using the following information.

House Value	Premium
<= €250000	0.1% of house value
€250001–€400000	0.2% of house value
> €400000	0.3% of house value

2. Calculate the contents premium using the following information.

Contents Value	Premium
<= €10000	0.5% of contents value
€10001–€15000	1.0% of contents value
€15001–€20000	1.5% of contents value
> € 20000	2.0% of contents value

3. Calculate the total premium.
4. Don't Riskit Insurance offers three methods of payment, as follows.

(a) Payment option A: payment in full at time of purchase
(b) Payment option B: 50% initial payment + remainder paid in 12 monthly instalments
(c) Payment option C: 12 monthly instalments, no payment up front.
5. Calculate the initial payment and monthly instalment for each client using separate IF functions (**Hint:** *If a client chooses payment option A, there would be no monthly instalments*).
6. Format all money amounts to currency.
7. Format the range A4:I13 using Autoformat, Classic 2.
8. Implement spreadsheet protection so that data can only be entered in the range A5:D13 and so that formulas and functions aren't displayed in the formula bar.
9. Rename Sheet1 as House Insurance.
10. Each of the clients listed Table 7.21 has also applied for car insurance. Enter the data displayed in Table 7.22 on page 138 in Sheet2 of the same workbook.
11. Enter linking formulas to read the client names from the House Insurance worksheet.
12. Calculate age premium using the following information.

Age of Client	Premium
<25	10% of car value
25–35	5% of car value
36–50	3% of car value
>50	2% of car value

13. Calculate the value premium using the following information.

Value of Car	Premium
<= €10000	1.0% of car value
€10001–€15000	1.5% of car value
€15001–€20000	2.0% of car value
>€20000	2.5% of car value

14. Cars insured in the Dublin area have an additional weighting of 0.5% of the car value. Calculate the Dublin weighting using an IF function.
15. Calculate the total premium.
16. Calculate the initial payment and monthly instalment using the payment options guidelines listed for household insurance.
17. Format all money amounts to currency.
18. Format the range A4:K13 using Autoformat, Classic 2.
19. Implement spreadsheet protection so that data can only be entered in the range B5:E13 and so that formulas and functions aren't displayed in the formula bar.
20. Rename Sheet2 as Car Insurance.
21. Enter data in Sheet3 as shown in Table 7.23 on page 139.
22. In column A enter linking formulas to read the client names from the House Insurance worksheet.
23. In B5 calculate the total premium by adding the total premium from the House Insurance worksheet to the total premium from the Car Insurance worksheet.

Table 7.22

	A	B	C	D	E	F	G	H	I	J	K
1					DON'T RISKIT INSURANCE						
2											
3					Motor Policies						
4	Client Name	Age	Value of Car	Dublin Area	Payment Option	Age Premium	Value Premium	Dublin Weighting	Total Premium	Initial Payment	Monthly Instalment
5		19	9000	Yes	C						
6		35	6500	No	A						
7		28	12500	Yes	A						
8		44	19000	Yes	C						
9		21	9500	Yes	B						
10		37	35000	Yes	B						
11		55	16000	No	C						
12		27	45000	Yes	A						
13		18	13000	No	B						

Table 7.23

	A	B	C	D
1	DON'T RISKIT INSURANCE			
2	Policy Report			
3				
4	Client Name	Total Premium	Total Initial Payment	Total Monthly Instalment
5				
6				
7				
8				
9				
10				
11				
12				
13				

24. In C5 calculate the total initial payment by adding the total initial payment from the House Insurance worksheet to the total initial payment from the Car Insurance worksheet.

25. In D5 calculate the total monthly instalment by adding the total monthly instalment from the House Insurance worksheet to the total monthly instalment from the Car Insurance worksheet.

26. Copy the summary formulas using fill down.

27. Format all money amounts to currency.

28. Format the range A4:D13 using Autoformat, Classic 2.

29. Implement spreadsheet protection so that data cannot be entered in this worksheet and so that all formulas are hidden.

30. Rename Sheet3 as Summary.

31. Delete all unused worksheets in the workbook.

32. Protect the workbook for structure and windows.

33. Save the spreadsheet as **House and Car Insurance**.

 ## Compound IF Function

There are two types of compound IF functions.

1. Compound IF where the true action is implemented only when all conditions are satisfied

2. Compound IF where the true action is implemented when one or more conditions are satisfied.

Compound IF Where All Conditions Must be Satisfied

This type of compound IF function is required where the IF function must decide to take one of two possible courses of action. The decision is based on multiple conditions. *When all the conditions are satisfied*, the first course of action is taken. The second course of action is taken when all of the conditions aren't satisfied.

A simple IF only allows us to have one condition. When there are two or more conditions we must use a function inside the condition section of the IF function. The function that we use depends on how many of the conditions must be satisfied. If the true action is dependent on *all of the conditions being satisfied* then we must use an **AND** function. If the true action is dependent on *some of the conditions being satisfied* then we must use an **OR** function. Because there are only two possible courses of action there is no need for nesting because only one IF function is required.

 Note: The word 'compound' indicates that each action depends on multiple conditions.

Calculating the Performance Premium

Returning to our Online Insurance Company spreadsheet we'll see how a compound IF function is used to calculate the performance premium.

Performance premium: Drivers with sports cars that have an engine capacity above 1600cc are charged 40% extra on the basic premium.

In this case, the IF function must decide if the client should be penalised for the performance of the car. This decision depends on two conditions: whether the engine capacity is above 1600cc and whether the car is a sports model. Because the true action is dependent on both conditions being satisfied, an AND function is required.

Analysing a Compound IF Where All Conditions Must be Satisfied

Two or more conditions (all of which must be satisfied): is the car a sports car, and is the engine capacity above 1600cc?

True action: Drivers of sports cars with engine capacities above 1600cc are charged 40% extra on the basic premium.

False action: Drivers of cars which don't satisfy both conditions aren't charged extra.

Structure of the Compound IF Function

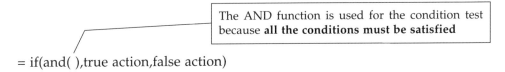

The AND function is used for the condition test because **all the conditions must be satisfied**

= if(and( ),true action,false action)

Table 7.24

	A	B	C	D	E	F
1				Basic Premium	€300	
2				Total Premium		
3	Policy Holder	Jim Collins				
4	Gender	Male	Gender Premium	€60		
5	Age	27	Age Premium	€30		
6	Full Drivers Licence	Yes	Performance Premium	=if(and(B8="Yes", B7>1600),E1*40%,0)		
7	Engine cc	1800				
8	Sports Model	Yes				
9	Claims to Date	0				

Writing the IF Function

In the spreadsheet displayed in Table 7.24, the task of the IF function is to check if the engine capacity entered in B7 is greater than 1600 and whether yes or no was entered in B8. The conditions and resulting actions are summarised in Table 7.25.

Table 7.25

Conditions (both of which must be satisfied)		Resulting Action
Engine cc	Sports Model	Performance Premium
>1600	Yes	40% of basic premium

Where both conditions aren't satisfied, the performance premium is zero. In this case, the number in B7 is greater than 1600 and yes was entered in B8 so the performance premium is calculated by multiplying E1 by 40%, giving 120. The IF function is entered in D6, as shown in Table 7.24.

Points to Note

1. The AND function is 'inside' the IF function and is used to carry out the two condition tests on which payment of the sports car premium depends. The bracket of the AND function must be closed off before completing the condition section of the IF function.

IF functions rule eight: Less than (<), less than or equal to (<=), equal to (=), greater than (>), greater than or equal to (>=) and not equal to (<>) should only be used in the condition section of the IF function. They *should not* be used in the true action or false action sections.

IF functions rule nine: Use of arithmetic operators + - * / within an AND/OR function is not recommended. It's best to do all of your calculations in separate cells and then refer to these cells using the AND/OR function.

Compound IF Where Some Conditions Must be Satisfied

This type of compound IF function is required where the IF function must decide to take one of two possible courses of action. The decision is based on multiple conditions. *Where at least one of the conditions is satisfied*, the first course of action is taken. The second course of action is taken when all of the conditions aren't satisfied.

Calculating the Claims Bonus

Returning to our Online Insurance Company spreadsheet, we'll see how a compound simple IF function is used to calculate the claims bonus.

Claims bonus: Drivers who are either over 30 or who have no previous claims are entitled to a reduction of 5% off the basic premium.

In this case, the IF function must decide if the client is entitled to a 5% bonus. This decision depends on two conditions: whether the driver is over 30 or whether the driver has no previous claims. Because the true action is dependant on at least one condition being satisfied, an OR function is required. (**Note:** *The true action will also be carried out if all conditions in an OR function are satisfied.*)

Analysing a Compound IF Where Some Conditions Must be Satisfied

Two or more conditions (at least one of which must be satisfied): is the driver over 30 or has the driver made no claims to date?

True action: Drivers who are over 30 **or** who have no previous claims are entitled to a reduction of 5% off the basic premium.

False action: Drivers under 30 with previous claims don't qualify for the reduction.

Structure of the Compound IF Function

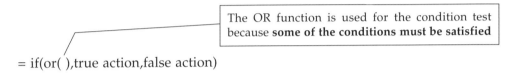

The OR function is used for the condition test because **some of the conditions must be satisfied**

= if(or( ),true action,false action)

Table 7.26

	A	B	C	D	E	F
1				**Basic Premium**	€300	
2				**Total Premium**		
3	**Policy Holder**	**Jim Collins**				
4	Gender	**Male**	Gender Premium	€60		
5	Age	27	Age Premium	€30		
6	Full Drivers Licence	**Yes**	Performance Premium	€120		
7	Engine cc	1800	Claims Bonus	**=if(or(B5>30,B9=0),E1*5%,0)**		
8	Sports Model	**Yes**				
9	Claims to Date	**0**				

Writing the IF Function

In the spreadsheet displayed in Table 7.26, the task of the IF function is to check if the age entered in B5 is greater than 30 or if the claims to date entered in B9 is zero. The conditions and resulting actions are summarised in Table 7.27 on page 144.
   Where neither of these conditions are satisfied, the claims bonus is zero.
   In this case the age in B5 is not greater than 30 but B9 is equal to zero so the claims bonus is calculated by multiplying E1 by 5%, giving 15. The IF function is entered in D7, as shown in Table 7.26 above.

Table 7.27

	Conditions (either of which must be satisfied)		Resulting Action
Age	Claims to date		Claims Bonus
>30	0		5% of basic premium

Compound IF Assignment One

Create a new spreadsheet workbook and enter the data shown in Table 7.28. Enter formulas and functions in the shaded cells to complete the spreadsheet.

Table 7.28

	A	B	C	D	E	F	G	H	I	J
	Name	Department	Salary	Weekly Pay	Week1 Hours	Week1 Bonus	Week1 Pay	Week2 Hours	Week2 Bonus	Week2 Pay
1										
2	A Arnold	Finance	40900		35			35		
3	B Burke	Marketing	37000		40			35		
4	C Cotton	Sales	24614		45			30		
5	D Eastwood	Finance	18000		35			35		
6	G Hunt	Sales	18000		30			22		
7	P Byrne	Sales	19640		35			50		
8	R Madigan	Marketing	17960		35			35		
9	F Fox	Sales	18350		20			40		
10	J Costello	Sales	20300		24			33		
11	B Galway	Sales	17260		40			24		
12	S Troy	Marketing	18416		35			27		
13	L Keane	Sales	21780		30			18		

1. Calculate weekly pay.

2. Employees in the sales department who work for more than 35 hours in any one week get a bonus of 20% of their weekly pay. Calculate the bonuses for Week1 and Week2. (**Hint:** *use an AND function within an IF function.*)

3. Week1 pay is weekly pay plus Week1 bonus. Create a similar formula to calculate Week2 pay.

4. Use conditional formatting to highlight bonus amounts.

Tip: Conditional formatting for Week1 bonuses can be copied to Week2 bonuses using the Format Painter.

5. Format all money amounts to currency.
6. Rename Sheet1 as Bonuses. Delete all unused worksheets in the workbook.
7. Implement spreadsheet protection so that data can only be entered in the ranges A2:C13, E2:E13 and H2:H13 and so that formulas and functions aren't displayed in the formula bar.

Tip: Multiple ranges can be highlighted by holding down the CTRL key when highlighting.

8. Print the Bonuses worksheet in landscape orientation with gridlines and row and column headings displayed.
9. Save the spreadsheet as **Weekly Payroll**.

Compound IF Assignment Two

Create a new spreadsheet workbook and enter the data shown in Table 7.29. Enter formulas and functions in the shaded cells to complete the spreadsheet.

Table 7.29

	A	B	C	D	E	F	G
1	Video Title	Day of Rental	Price per Night	Days Rented	Total	Special Offer	Amount Payable
2	American Pie 2	Monday	3.5	1			
3	Jeepers Creepers	Monday	4.5	1			
4	Legally Blonde	Monday	4.5	1			
5	Driven	Tuesday	4.5	1			
6	Scary Movie 2	Tuesday	3.5	2			
7	The Fast and Furious	Wednesday	4.5	1			
8	Swordfish	Wednesday	4.5	2			
9	Moulin Rouge	Wednesday	4.5	2			
10	A Knight's Tale	Wednesday	3.5	1			
11	Angel Eyes	Thursday	4.5	2			
12	The Forsaken	Thursday	4.5	1			
13	Traffic	Friday	3.5	1			

(Contd.)

Table **7.29** (*Contd.*)

	A	B	C	D	E	F	G
14	Original Sin	Friday	4.5	1			
15	The Others	Friday	4.5	1			
16	The Animal	Saturday	4.5	2			
17	Harry Potter	Saturday	4.5	2			
18	Persuasion	Saturday	4.5	1			
19	Kiss of the Dragon	Sunday	3.5	1			
20	Ghosts of Mars	Sunday	4.5	2			

1. Calculate the total.
2. Calculate special offer. There's a reduction of 50% off the total on all videos rented on Monday, Tuesday or Wednesday.
3. Calculate the amount payable.
4. Format all money amounts to currency.
5. Use conditional formatting to display special offer amounts in red, bold italics.
6. Rename sheet1 as Rentals. Delete all other worksheets in the workbook.
7. Implement spreadsheet protection so that data can only be entered in the range A2:D20 and so that formulas and functions aren't displayed in the formula bar.
8. Save the spreadsheet as **Video Offer**.

 Compound IF Assignment Three

Create a new spreadsheet workbook and enter the data shown in Table 7.30. Enter functions in the shaded cells to complete the spreadsheet.

Table **7.30**

	A	B	C	D	E
1	Model	Processor Speed	RAM	Hard Disk Size	Scrap?
2	Dell P100t	100	64	540	
3	Dell P75t	75	24	540	
4	Acer 25sx	25	12	240	
5	Acer 33sx	33	12	201	
6	Dell P75t	75	16	250	
7	ASTG P1a	150	32	1280	
8	Acer 66dx	66	12	201	
9	ASTG P1	120	16	1280	

1. Determine which PCs should be scrapped using an IF function. (All PCs with processor speeds less than 50 Mhz, less than 16 Mb RAM and hard disks under 500 Mb are to be scrapped. The IF function should display Yes if the PC is to be scrapped and No if it isn't for scrap.)

2. Use conditional formatting to highlight the models that are to be scrapped in red, bold italics.

3. Sort the data in ascending order of model.

4. Create a stacked column chart to display data in the range A1:D9 where hard disk size, RAM and processor speed are represented by column sections. The chart title is Hardware Specifications. The title for the y axis is Mb. The chart should be on a separate chart sheet named Performance Chart.

5. Rename Sheet1 as List of PCs. Delete all unused worksheets in the workbook.

6. Save the spreadsheet as **To Scrap or Not To Scrap**.

Compound IF Assignment Four

Create a new spreadsheet workbook and enter the data shown in Table 7.31. Enter functions in the shaded cells to complete the spreadsheet.

Table 7.31

	A	B	C	D
1	**Passenger Name**	**Age**	**Destination**	**Passenger Load Fee**
2	Tom Tiernan	25	Atlanta	
3	Alison Byrne	10	Atlanta	
4	Conor Callaghan	52	Chicago	
5	Bill Murphy	8	Paris	
6	Kevin O Leary	11	New York	
7	Sue Dunne	19	London	
8	Miriam Delaney	21	Boston	
9	Denis Langton	33	Brussels	
10	Maeve Twomey	20	Boston	
11	Garret O Neill	7	Boston	
12	Nora Evans	15	London	
13	Evelyn Sheehy	57	New York	
14	Tim Mooney	16	Chicago	
15	Cathy Burke	48	Atlanta	

1. Calculate the passenger load fee. This is €7.23 on the New York, Boston, Atlanta and Chicago routes. On all other routes the passenger load fee is €3.95.

2. Format all money amounts to currency.

3. Sort the data in ascending order of destination.

4. Rename Sheet1 as Passenger Load Fees. Delete all other worksheets in the workbook.

5. Implement spreadsheet protection so that data can only be entered in the range A2:C15 and so that formulas and functions aren't displayed in the formula bar.

6. Save the spreadsheet as **Airline Fees**.

Nested Compound IF Function

A nested compound IF function is required where the IF function must decide to take one of three or more possible courses of action. Each decision is based on multiple conditions. Depending on the nature of the conditions the course of action taken will the one for which some or all the conditions are satisfied.

Calculating the Licence Bonus

Returning to our Online Insurance Company spreadsheet, we'll see how a nested compound IF function is used to calculate the licence bonus.

Licence bonus:

- Full licence holders aged 18 or under get a reduction of 1% of the basic premium
- Full licence holders aged between 19 and 21 inclusive get a reduction of 2% of the basic premium
- Full licence holders aged between 22 and 25 inclusive get a reduction of 3% of the basic premium
- Full licence holders aged between 26 and 70 inclusive get a reduction of 5% of the basic premium
- No bonus is given to drivers who don't hold a full licence or to drivers aged 71 or older.

In a nested compound IF function there are three or more possible courses of action. In this case there are five possible courses of action: a bonus of 1%, 2%, 3% or 5% can be given to drivers who hold a full licence, depending on their age. Each bonus depends on both conditions being satisfied. For this reason AND functions are required. The fifth course of action is that no bonus will be given to drivers who don't hold a full licence or to drivers aged 71 or older.

Structure of the Nested Compound IF Function

=if(and( ), action1, if(and( ), action2, action3))

 Note: Conditions in a nested compound IF function may require AND functions, OR functions or a combination of both. The number of conditions will vary according to the number of possible courses of action. Excel allows a maximum of seven IFs nested inside the first IF.

Table 7.32

	A	B	C	D	E	F
1				Basic Premium	€300	
2				Total Premium	=E1+sum(D4:D6)-D7-D8	
3	Policy Holder	Jim Collins				
4	Gender	Male	Gender Premium	€60		
5	Age	27	Age Premium	€30		
6	Full Drivers Licence	Yes	Performance Premium	€120		
7	Engine cc	1800	Claims Bonus	€15		
8	Sports Model	Yes	Licence Bonus	=if(and(B5<=18,B6="Yes"), E1*1%,if(and(B5<=21, B6="Yes"),E1*2%,if(and(B5<=25,B6="Yes") E1*3%,if(and(B5<=70,B6="Yes"),E1*5%,0))))		
9	Claims to Date	0				

Writing the IF Function

In the spreadsheet displayed in Table 7.32, the task of the IF function is to check the age that was entered in B5 and, in relation to full drivers licence, whether yes or no was entered in B6. The conditions and resulting actions are summarised in Table 7.33 on page 150.

No bonus is given to drivers who don't hold a full licence or to drivers aged 71 or older.

In this case the age in B5 is between 26 and 70 inclusive and B6 equals "Yes", so the licence bonus is calculated by multiplying E1 by 5%, giving 15. The IF function is entered in D8, as shown above in Table 7.32.

The Online Insurance spreadsheet can be completed by entering a formula in E2 to calculate the total premium. Once the spreadsheet is completed it will instantly calculate the total premium based on data entered in the range B4:B9. In this case the total premium is €480.

Table 7.33

	Conditions (both of which must be satisfied)		Resulting Action
	Age	Full Drivers Licence	Licence Bonus
1	<=18	Yes	1% of basic premium
2	19–21 *inclusive*	Yes	2% of basic premium
3	22–25 *inclusive*	Yes	3% of basic premium
4	26–70 *inclusive*	Yes	5% of basic premium

Nested Compound IF Assignment One

Create a new spreadsheet workbook and enter the data shown in Table 7.34. Enter formulas and functions in the shaded cells to complete the spreadsheet.

Table 7.34

	A	B	C	D	E	F	G	H
1	Depart Date	Return Date	Name	Miles	Conference	Number of Nights	Hotel Expenses	Special Expenses
2	01/05/2003	05/05/2003	Lisa Barrett	168	Yes			
3	04/05/2003	06/05/2003	Mark Smith	57	No			
4	12/05/2003	12/05/2003	Gerry Dunne	129	Yes			
5	13/05/2003	14/05/2003	John Meadows	81	Yes			
6	13/05/2003	17/05/2003	Caroline Murphy	63	No			
7	14/05/2003	14/05/2003	Lucy O Neill	205	Yes			
8	18/05/2003	24/05/2003	Sam Hartnett	188	No			

1. Calculate the number of nights in each trip.

Tip: When you refer to dates or times in a calculation, the result may be displayed in Date/Time format. Click the Comma Style button to display the result as a number.

Comma Style button

Figure 7.7

2. Calculate hotel expenses using the following information: there are no hotel expenses for people who return on the same day. For people who stay overnight, hotel expenses are paid at €90 per night.

3. Special expenses are paid on the following basis: people who attend a conference and travel more than 200 miles are entitled to €100. Those who attend a conference and travel between 150 and 200 miles inclusive are entitled to €50. People who travel less than 150 miles aren't entitled to special expenses regardless of whether or not they attend a conference.

4. Format all money amounts to currency.

5. Sort the data in descending order of miles.

6. Use conditional formatting to emphasise the names of those entitled to special expenses in red, bold italics.

7. Implement spreadsheet protection so that data can only be entered in the range A2:E8 and so that formulas and functions aren't displayed in the formula bar.

8. Rename Sheet1 as Expense Claims. Delete all other worksheets in the workbook.

9. Save the spreadsheet as **Employee Travel**.

 Nested Compound IF Assignment Two

Create a new spreadsheet workbook and enter the data shown in Table 7.35.

Table 7.35

	A	B
1	Colour Predictor	
2		
3	Enter first colour	
4		
5	Enter second colour	
6		
7	Resulting colour	

1. In B7 create an IF function that will predict the colour when any of the five colour combinations listed below is entered in cells B3 and B5, respectively.

- Red and white gives pink
- Red and yellow gives orange
- Red and blue gives purple
- Yellow and blue gives green
- Red and green gives brown.

Where no colours are entered the IF function should display the text 'Enter Colours'.

Test the IF function by entering red in B3 and white in B5. Pink should then be displayed in B7. Continue testing the IF function for all colour combinations listed above.

2. Implement spreadsheet protection so that data can only be entered in B3 and B5 and so that the function in B7 is not displayed in the formula bar.

3. Rename Sheet1 as Mix Colours. Delete all other worksheets in the workbook.

4. Save the spreadsheet as **Colour Predictor**.

Tip: Before you create an IF function make a note of the number of possible courses of action that can be implemented by the function. Then determine how many conditions each course of action is dependent on. This helps you to focus in your mind how many IFs are required and whether you need to use AND/OR functions in the conditions.

 Nested Compound IF Assignment Three

Create a new spreadsheet workbook and enter the data shown in Table 7.36. Enter formulas and functions in the shaded cells to complete the spreadsheet.

Table 7.36

	A	B	C	D	E	F
1	Employee Name	Car	Engine Size	Distance	Rate	Total
2	Stephen Aherne	Yaris	1.0	8350		
3	Jane Dineen	Colt	1.3	8200		
4	Maurice Ryan	Mondeo	1.6	15890		
5	Denis Kinsella	Fiesta	1.1	9850		
6	Avril Byrne	Mazda 626	1.8	10340		
7	Francis Keane	Focus	1.4	7001		
8	Paul Walsh	Passat	1.8	2598		

1. Calculate the rate using the following information.

- The rate is €0.75 for cars with an engine size of 1.1 or less that travelled less than 10,000 miles
- The rate is €0.85 for cars with an engine size between 1.2 and 1.6 inclusive that travelled less than 10,000 miles
- The rate is €0.95 for cars with an engine size between 1.7 and 3.0 inclusive that travelled less than 10,000 miles

- The rate for all other combinations of engine size and distance is €0.65.

2. Calculate the total.
3. Format engine sizes to display one decimal place.
4. Format all money amounts to currency.
5. Sort the data in descending order of total.
6. Display the expenses claimed by all employees using a pie chart. The chart title is Breakdown of Expenses. Display the value corresponding to each slice of the pie. Display the pie chart on a separate chart sheet named Expense Chart. (**Hint**: *You'll have to highlight two separate ranges.*)
7. In Sheet1 implement spreadsheet protection so that data can only be entered in the range A2:D8 and so that formulas and functions aren't displayed in the formula bar.
8. Rename Sheet1 as Travel Expenses. Delete all unused worksheets in the workbook.
9. Save the spreadsheet as **Mileage Allowances**.

Working with Time Values in Excel

When you enter a time such as 18:00 in a spreadsheet cell, this isn't what's actually stored in the cell. When a time is entered in an Excel spreadsheet it's stored as a decimal fraction between zero and one.

Examples of Time Values in Excel

Table 7.37

Time entered in cell	Value stored in cell
00:01	0.000694444444444444
01:00	0.0416666666666667
02:00	0.0833333333333333
05:00	0.208333333333333
10:00	0.416666666666667
15:00	0.625
18:00	0.75
22:00	0.916666666666667
23:00	0.958333333333333
23:59	0.999305555555556

Shown in Table 7.37 on page 153 are the values corresponding to times entered in an Excel spreadsheet. When you enter a time, Excel stores a decimal number in the cell corresponding to that time but displays the decimal number in Time Format. For example, if you type 18:00 in A1, Excel stores 0.75 in A1 but displays 18:00. A time can be displayed as a decimal number by clicking the Comma Style button.

The decimal number equivalents of times range from zero to 0.9999999, representing the times from 0:00:00 to 23:59:59.

This discrepancy between the cell display (18:00) and the cell contents (0.75) can cause problems when referring to cells containing times with formulas or functions.

For example, the spreadsheet displayed in Table 7.38 calculates the cost of mobile phone calls depending on the duration of the call and the time the call was made. Calls made before 18:00 cost €0.60 per minute. Calls made from 18:00 onwards cost €0.20 per minute.

Table 7.38

	A	B	C	D
1	Time of Call	Duration (minutes)	Unit Cost	Total Cost
2	14:55	0.5		
3	17:01	6.0		
4	18:20	21.2		
5	19:56	35.6		
6	21:09	12.0		

The unit cost is calculated using an IF function. This IF function needs to refer to the time 18:00 so that it can apply the higher rate to calls made before 18:00 and the lower rate to calls made from 18:00 onwards. However, Excel doesn't recognise 18:00 as a value. If we were to create an IF function in C2 to calculate the unit cost as =if(A2<18:00,0.6,0.2), then Excel would display an error message. Instead of referring to 18:00 in the function we need to refer to the decimal equivalent of 18:00, which is 0.75. So the correct IF function would be =if(A2<0.75,0.6,0.2).

There are two problems with using decimal time equivalents in formulas and functions.

1. Formulas and functions that contain decimal time equivalents are difficult to understand
2. Because some decimal time equivalents have up to 18 places of decimals, it's easy to make a mistake when entering them in formulas and functions.

The solution is to enter each time that a formula or function must refer to in a separate cell. Instead of referring to the decimal time equivalent, refer to the cell containing the relevant time. Better still, assign a name to each cell containing a time. Assuming that 18:00 in entered in A1 of Sheet2 and that this cell has been assigned the name sixpm, we can rewrite our IF function as follows: =if(A2<sixpm,0.6,0.2).

The function is now easier to understand and there is no need to use decimal time equivalents.

Exercise

Complete the spreadsheet displayed in Table 7.38 on page 154 as follows.

1. Enter 18:00 in cell A1 of Sheet2. Assign the name sixpm to this cell.
2. Create an IF function in cell C2 of Sheet1 to calculate the unit cost (calls made before 18:00 cost 0.60 per minute, calls made from 18:00 onwards cost €0.20 per minute). The function should refer to the cell name sixpm.
3. The total cost is duration (minutes) multiplied by unit cost.
4. Format all money amounts to currency.
5. Save the spreadsheet as **Mobile Phone Bill**.

Nested Compound IF Assignment Four

Create a new spreadsheet workbook and enter the data shown in Table 7.39. Enter formulas and functions in the shaded cells to complete the spreadsheet.

1. Enter 15:00 in A1 of Sheet2. Assign the name threepm to this cell. Enter 17:30 in A2 of Sheet2. Assign the name fivethirty to this cell. Enter 18:00 in A3 of Sheet2. Assign the name sixpm to this cell.
2. Calculate price. This price is €4.00 for films shown before 15:00, €5.00 for films shown between 15:00 and 18:00 and €6.00 for films shown after 18:00. (**Hint:** *Refer to the cells named threepm and sixpm in the function.*)

Tip: Don't enclose cell names in inverted commas when referring to them in functions as this causes Excel to treat them as text instead of references to specific cells.

3. Calculate the total.
4. A 10% discount is given to groups of 15 or more in screens one and two for the 17:30 show. (**Hint:** *Refer to the cell named fivethirty using a combination of IF, OR and AND functions.*)
5. Calculate the amount due.
6. Format all money amounts to currency.
7. Use conditional formatting to emphasise the film names and group discount amounts in red, bold italics for all films where the group discount applies.
8. Implement spreadsheet protection so that data can only be entered in the ranges A2:D16 and F2:F16 and so that formulas and functions aren't displayed in the formula bar.
9. Rename Sheet1 as Group Discounts.
10. Rename Sheet2 as Cell Names.
11. Delete all unused worksheets in the workbook.

Table 7.39

	A	B	C	D	E	F	G	H	I
1	Screen Number	Film	Date	Time	Price	Group Size	Total	Group Discount	Amount Due
2	1	About a Boy	26/9/2003	14:00		10			
3	2	The Royal Tenenbaums	26/9/2003	14:00		25			
4	3	Lord of the Rings	26/9/2003	14:00		12			
5	4	A Beautiful Mind	26/9/2003	14:00		18			
6	5	The Scorpion King	26/9/2003	14:00		30			
7	1	About a Boy	26/9/2003	17:30		20			
8	2	The Royal Tenenbaums	26/9/2003	17:30		16			
9	3	Lord of the Rings	26/9/2003	17:30		35			
10	4	A Beautiful Mind	26/9/2003	17:30		12			
11	5	The Scorpion King	26/9/2003	17:30		20			
12	1	About a Boy	26/9/2003	20:45		5			
13	2	The Royal Tenenbaums	26/9/2003	20:45		15			
14	3	Lord of the Rings	26/9/2003	20:45		23			
15	4	A Beautiful Mind	26/9/2003	20:45		20			
16	5	The Scorpion King	26/9/2003	20:45		8			

12. Print the Group Discounts worksheet.
13. Save the spreadsheet as **Cinema Attendance**.

 Tip: Pressing the F3 key displays a list of all cell and range names contained in your spreadsheet.

Toolbar Buttons Introduced in Chapter Seven

To center a heading within a range of cells, first highlight the cells and then click the Merge and Centre button. The heading must be in the first cell of the highlighted range.

Figure 7.8   The **Merge and Center** button

To remove percentage, currency or date and time formats from numbers in a cell or range of cells, click the Comma Style button. Any formats will be removed and the cell contents will be displayed as pure numbers. Commas will be included in numbers greater than 9999, e.g. 10,000.

Figure 7.9   The **Comma Style** button

Additional Points Concerning IF Functions

1. Once you have created an IF function, test it by entering different values in the cell or cells that the IF function refers to. For example, where an IF function applies a discount to children under 12 based on an age entered in B2, test the IF function by entering a number less than 12 in B2. Does the IF function calculate a discount? Does it calculate the discount correctly? Now enter a number greater than 12 in B2. The discount should now be zero. All IF functions should be tested in this way.

2. More complex IF functions should be planned before they are attempted. Use the following checklist.

Table 7.40

Number of actions?	
How many conditions does each action depend on?	
If there are multiple conditions, are conditions linked or independent of each other?	

The answers to these questions will determine the structure of the IF function.

3. Finally, where an IF function is very complex, break it down into steps. A very complex calculation can often be carried out in two or more steps. Approaching complex calculations in this way will make your spreadsheets easier to use and understand in the long run.

8

Lookup Functions

In Chapter 8, you will learn how to

- Store data in a lookup table
- Use lookup functions to reference data stored in a lookup table.

Imagine you work in a company that supplies office equipment and stationery. The company has a total of 1,000 items in stock. Details of the items are kept in a price list. Each item has a number, e.g. item no. 1, item no. 2, item no. 3 to item no. 1000, as shown in Table 8.1.

Table 8.1

Office Supplies		
Price List		
Item Number	**Description**	**Price**
1	Appointments Book	€18.93
2	Telephone Calls Book	€14.66
3	Postages Book	€13.33
4	Time Book	€9.56
5	Petty Cash Book	€21.60
6	A4 Analysis Pads(5)	€4.22
7	Twinlock Accounts Book	€19.75
256	Post-It Notes	€7.50
998	Crocodile Clip Badge(25)	€28.10
999	Universal Name Badge(5)	€4.21
1000	Visitors Badge(25)	€43.96

In your capacity as accounts executive, other members of staff frequently ask you questions such as 'what's the price of item 256?' Each time you're asked a question like this, you get out the price list and look down through the first column until you find the number (in this case 256). Looking across to the next column, you see that item 256 is Post-It Notes. Then you look across to the next column to find the price, which is €7.50.

In any process where data is stored in a list and that list is constantly referred to, lookup functions can be used to speed up the process of retrieving data from the list. The lookup function works in a way that is very similar to the process of manually looking up a list, as described above. First, the information about products and prices would be stored in a special area in the spreadsheet, known as a lookup table. The first column (item number) is used as a reference to locate specific items in the table. Once an item is located, the spreadsheet can read all the information relating to that item.

There are two types of lookup tables: vertical lookup tables and horizontal lookup tables.

Vertical Lookup Tables

In a vertical lookup table the information is set up in columns. When looking for the price of item 256, *you must look down* the first column to find 256 *and then across* to the third column to find the price.

Table 8.2

Item Number	Description	Price
1	Appointments Book	€18.93
2	Telephone Calls Book	€14.66
3	Postages Book	€13.33
4	Time Book	€9.56
5	Petty Cash Book	€21.60
6	A4 Analysis Pads(5)	€4.22
7	Twinlock Accounts Book	€19.75
256	Post-It Notes	€7.50
998	Crocodile Clip Badge(25)	€28.10
999	Universal Name Badge(5)	€4.21
1000	Visitors Badge(25)	€43.96

Rule: For vertical lookup tables, the first column must be in ascending alphabetical or ascending numerical order.

Horizontal Lookup Tables

In a horizontal lookup table the information is set up in rows. When looking for the price of item 256, *you must look across* the first row to find 256 *and then down* to the third row to find the price.

Table 8.3

Item Number	1	2	3	4	→	256
Description	Appointments Book	Telephone Calls Book	Postages Book	Time Book	→	Post-It Notes
Price	€18.93	€14.66	€13.33	€9.56	→	€7.50

 Rule: For horizontal lookup tables, the top row must be in ascending alphabetical or ascending numerical order.

Horizontal and vertical lookup tables work in the same way and will give the same answer when used correctly. Which one you use depends on the layout of your spreadsheet, the data you're storing and your own personal preference.

Lookup tables save time and reduce errors. They eliminate the need to look through paper-based lists to find information relating to a particular item. Instead, this work is done by the lookup function. Secondly, updates or changes made to data stored in the lookup table are automatically recognised by the lookup function. In a retail spreadsheet application this would greatly reduce the chance of a customer being charged the wrong price. Sales staff wouldn't have to remember price changes. The prices can be stored in a lookup table. Once the bar code for a particular product is entered in the spreadsheet, the lookup function can find the price relating to that bar code. Usually, one member of staff would be given the responsibility for updating prices in the lookup table. As long as the sales staff enter the correct bar code at the point of sale, the up-to-date price for a particular product will be found by the lookup function.

 ## Vertical Lookup Tables – Worked Example

In this example we will use a vertical lookup table to store product descriptions and prices.

Step One – Set Up the Lookup Table

The lookup table will contain information about products and prices that will be frequently referred to. The best method is to set up the lookup table in a separate worksheet because this makes the spreadsheet less cluttered and easier to work with.

Enter the information that's frequently referred to in Sheet1 of a new spreadsheet workbook, as shown in Table 8.4.

Table 8.4

	A	B	C
1	Item Number	Description	Price
2	1	Appointments Book	18.93
3	2	Telephone Calls Book	14.66
4	3	Postages Book	13.33
5	4	Time Book	9.56
6	5	Petty Cash Book	21.60
7	6	A4 Analysis Pads(5)	4.22
8	7	Twinlock Accounts Book	19.75
9	256	Post-It Notes	7.50
10	998	Crocodile Clip Badge(25)	28.10
11	999	Universal Name Badge(5)	4.21
12	1000	Visitors Badge(25)	43.96

Rename Sheet1 as Stock and format the prices to currency.

Step Two – Name the Lookup Table

We will assign the name pricelist to the lookup table. Highlight everything except the first row (A2:C12), as shown in Figure 8.1 on page 162.

Once you've highlighted the data contained in the lookup table, you must name this range by entering a name (in this case pricelist) in the Name Box and then pressing Enter, as shown in Figure 8.2 on page 162.

 Note: The first row isn't included in the lookup table because it doesn't contain data that will be referred to.

Excel will now recognise the range named pricelist as a vertical lookup table.

Now that we've set up the lookup table, we can refer to it for price and product information.

	A	B	C	D
1	Item Number	Description	Price	
2	1	Appointments Book	€ 18.93	
3	2	Telephone Calls Book	€ 14.66	
4	3	Postages Book	€ 13.33	
5	4	Time Book	€ 9.56	
6	5	Petty Cash Book	€ 21.60	
7	6	A4 Analysis Pads(5)	€ 4.22	
8	7	Twinlock Accounts Book	€ 19.75	
9	256	Post-It Notes	€ 7.50	
10	998	Crocodile Clip Badge(25)	€ 28.10	
11	999	Universal Name Badge(5)	€ 4.21	
12	1000	Visitors Badge(25)	€ 43.96	
13				

Figure 8.1

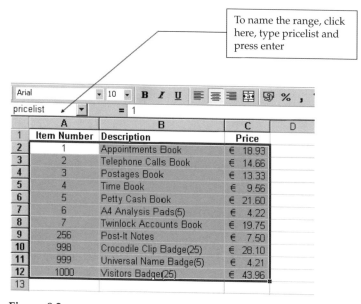

To name the range, click here, type pricelist and press enter

Figure 8.2

Step Three – Enter Data that Refers to Information Stored in the Lookup Table in a Separate Worksheet

Enter the data displayed in Table 8.5 on page 163 in Sheet2, then rename Sheet2 as Sales.

Details of items sold are displayed in Table 8.5. Each item number refers back to data stored in the lookup table, e.g. 998 is Crocodile Clip Badge, 4 refers to Time Book, etc. In step four, we will create lookup functions that will find the description and the price relating to each item number.

Step Four – Create the Lookup Function

Each product sold is identified by an item number. We can see in the spreadsheet displayed in Table 8.5 that five of item 998 and 100 of item 4 were sold, and so on.

Table 8.5

	A	B	C	D	E
1	Sales Records				
2					
3	Item No	Quantity	Description	Price	Total
4	998	5			
5	4	100			
6	6	25			
7	256	10			
8	1000	1			
9	999	5			
10	1	1			
11	7	20			
12	3	1			

We'll use lookup functions to find the information relating to each item number in the lookup table. So for example, one lookup function will tell us that item 998 is a Crocodile Clip Badge(25) and another lookup function will tell us that the price of this product is €28.10. There are two types of lookup functions: the VLOOKUP function and the HLOOKUP function. With a vertical lookup table, you must use a VLOOKUP function. With a horizontal lookup table, you must use a HLOOKUP function. As we're using a vertical lookup table we'll use a VLOOKUP function. Our first lookup function will be entered in C4 in the worksheet named Sales. It will find the description relating to item number 998.

Each lookup function contains three sections, separated by commas.

=VLOOKUP(1, 2, 3)

"1" This is the value we want to find a match for in the lookup table. The first item number that we're looking for is 998, stored in cell A4 in the Sales worksheet. We can complete the first section of the lookup function as follows: =vlookup(A4,

"2" This is where we refer to the lookup table itself. We've already given the name pricelist to the lookup table. We can complete the second section of the lookup function as follows: =vlookup(A4,pricelist,

"3" This is where we identify the column of the lookup table that contains the information we require. We're using a vertical lookup table that has three columns. Column one stores the item number, column two stores the description and column three stores the price. In this example we're looking for the description so we use the number 2 to identify column two. We can now complete the lookup function as follows: **=vlookup(A4,pricelist,2)**.

By typing this formula in cell C4, the spreadsheet will display the text Crocodile Clip Badge(25), which is the description of item 998. This function can be copied down to find the descriptions of the other items, as shown in Table 8.6.

Table 8.6

	A	B	C	D	E	F
1	Sales Records					
2						
3	Item No	Quantity	Description	Price	Total	
4	998	5	=vlookup(A4,pricelist,2) finds Crocodile Clip Badge(25)			
5	4	100	=vlookup(A5,pricelist,2) finds Time Book			
6	6	25	=vlookup(A6,pricelist,2) finds A4 Analysis Pads(5)			
7	256	10	=vlookup(A7,pricelist,2) finds Post-It Notes			
8	1000	1	=vlookup(A8,pricelist,2) finds Visitors Badge(25)			
9	999	5	=vlookup(A9,pricelist,2) finds Universal Name Badge(5)			
10	1	1	=vlookup(A10,pricelist,2) finds Appointments Book			
11	7	20	=vlookup(A11,pricelist,2) finds Twinlock Accounts Book			
12	3	1	=vlookup(A12,pricelist,2) finds Postages Book			

Creating a Lookup Function to Find the Price

This lookup function is very similar to the first one except that in this case the information we require is in column three instead of column two.

Step one: (set up the lookup table):*already complete*
Step two: (name the lookup table): *already complete*
Step three: (enter data that refers to the lookup table): *already complete*
Step four: create a lookup function to find the price, which is stored in column three of the lookup table.

This gives the following lookup function: =vlookup(a4,pricelist,3) as shown in Table 8.7 on page 165.

We can complete the exercise by entering a simple formula to calculate the total as shown in Table 8.8 on page 165. Save this spreadsheet as **Office Supplies**.

 Note: You can also write a lookup function without naming the lookup table. However, this isn't recommended as it makes the lookup function

Table 8.7

	A	B	C	D	E	F
1	Sales Records					
2						
3	Item No	Quantity	Description	Price	Total	
4	998	5	Crocodile Clip Badge(25)	=vlookup(A4, pricelist,3) finds €28.10		
5	4	100	Time Book	=vlookup(A5, pricelist,3) finds €9.56		
6	6	25	A4 Analysis Pads(5)	=vookup(A6, pricelist,3) finds €4.22		
7	256	10	Post-It Notes	=vlookup(A7, pricelist,3) finds €7.50		
8	1000	1	Visitors Badge(25)	=vlookup(A8, pricelist,3) finds €43.96		
9	999	5	Universal Name Badge(5)	=vlookup(A9, pricelist,3) finds €4.21		
10	1	1	Appointments Book	=vlookup(A10, pricelist,3) finds €18.93		
11	7	20	Twinlock Accounts Book	=vlookup(A11, pricelist,3) finds €19.75		
12	3	1	Postages Book	=vlookup(A12, pricelist,3) finds €13.33		

Table 8.8

	A	B	C	D	E
1	Sales Records				
2					
3	Item No	Quantity	Description	Price	Total
4	998	5	Crocodile Clip Badge(25)	€28.10	=D4*B4
5	4	100	Time Book	€9.56	=D5*B5
6	6	25	A4 Analysis Pads(5)	€4.22	=D6*B6
7	256	10	Post-It Notes	€7.50	=D7*B7
8	1000	1	Visitors Badge(25)	€43.96	=D8*B8
9	999	5	Universal Name Badge(5)	€4.21	=D9*B9
10	1	1	Appointments Book	€18.93	=D10*B10
11	7	20	Twinlock Accounts Book	€19.75	=D11*B11
12	3	1	Postages Book	€13.33	=D12*B12

more difficult to interpret. If we didn't name the lookup table, the lookup function would be_=vlookup(A4,Stock!A2:C12,2). It's also more difficult to copy a lookup function using this method.

Horizontal Lookup Tables – Worked Example

In this example we'll use a horizontal lookup table to store contact information for a sales representative.

Step One – Set Up the Lookup Table

This lookup table will contain information about sales contacts and distances that will be frequently referred to.

Enter the information that's frequently referred to in Sheet1 of a new spreadsheet workbook, as shown in Table 8.9, and rename Sheet1 as Clients.

Table 8.9

	A	B	C	D	E	F
1	Location	Gort	Headford	Loughrea	Oughterard	Tuam
2	Contact	Mark O Shea	Peter Flynn	Sue Barrett	Tina Moore	John Lynch
3	Distance	19	16	28	15	22

Step Two – Name the Lookup Table

Assign the name distances to the range B1:F3.

Step Three – Enter Data that Refers to Information Stored in the Lookup Table in a Separate Worksheet

Enter the data displayed in Table 8.10 on page 167 in Sheet2 and rename Sheet2 as Sales Trips.

Details of sales trips are displayed in Table 8.10. Each location name refers back to data stored in the lookup table, e.g. John Lynch is the contact in Tuam and the distance is 22 miles, Peter Flynn is the contact in Headford and the distance is 16 miles, etc. In step four, we'll create a lookup function that will find the contact relating to each location.

Step Four – Create the Lookup Function

Each contact is identified by the location name. Because we're using a horizontal

Table 8.10

	A	B	C	D	E
1		**Rate per Mile**	0.75		
2					
3	**Date**	**Location**	**Contact**	**Distance**	**Expenses**
4	04/08/2003	Tuam			
5	04/08/2003	Headford			
6	05/08/2003	Loughrea			
7	05/08/2003	Gort			
8	05/08/2003	Oughterard			

lookup table, we must use a HLOOKUP function to display the contact for each location. This lookup function will be entered in C4 in the worksheet named Sales Trips. It will find the contact name relating to Tuam.

The horizontal lookup function contains three sections, separated by commas.

=HLOOKUP(1, 2, 3)

"1" This is the value we want to find a match for in the lookup table. The first location that we're looking for is Tuam, which is stored in cell B4 in the Sales Trips worksheet. We can complete the first section of the lookup function as follows: =hlookup(B4,

"2" This is where we refer to the lookup table itself. We've already given the name distances to the lookup table. We can complete the second section of the lookup function as follows: =hlookup(B4,distances,

"3" This is where we identify the row of the lookup table that contains the information we require. We are using a horizontal lookup table that has three rows. Row one stores the location, row two stores the contact and row three stores the distance. In this case we are looking for the contact so we use the number 2 to identify column two. We can now complete the lookup function as follows:

=hlookup (B4, distances, 2).

By typing this formula in cell C4 the spreadsheet will display the text John Lynch, who is the contact in Tuam. This function can be copied down to find the contacts in the other locations, as shown in Table 8.11 on page 168.

Complete the spreadsheet as follows.

1. Create lookup functions to find the distance to each location.
2. Calculate expenses.

Table 8.11

	A	B	C	D	E
1		Rate per Mile	0.75		
2					
3	Date	Location	Contact	Distance	Expenses
4	04/08/2003	Tuam	=hlookup(B4,distances,2) finds John Lynch		
5	04/08/2003	Headford	=hlookup(B5,distances,2) finds Peter Flynn		
6	05/08/2003	Loughrea	=hlookup(B6,distances,2) finds Sue Barrett		
7	05/08/2003	Gort	=hlookup(B7,distances,2) finds Mark O Shea		
8	05/08/2003	Oughterard	=hlookup(B8,distances,2) finds Tina Moore		

Tip: The formula for expenses is easier to copy if you use a cell name for C1.

3. Save the spreadsheet as **Record of Sales Trips**.

Lookup Functions Assignment One

The data displayed in Table 8.12 relates to phone calls made by four people who rent a house together. In this assignment you will create a spreadsheet that will calculate how much each person should pay towards the phone bill.

1. Create a new spreadsheet workbook and rename Sheet1 as Telephone List.
2. Enter the data shown in Table 8.12 on page 169 in the worksheet named Telephone List.
3. Assign the name **phonenumbers** to an appropriate range of cells.
4. Sort the data in ascending order of number.
5. Rename Sheet2 as Telephone Bill.
6. Enter the data displayed in Table 8.13 on page 170 in the worksheet named Telephone Bill.
7. Create lookup functions to find the person called and the caller for each number dialled. (**Hint:** These lookup functions should refer to the range named phonenumbers.)

The number 6042221 was incorrectly entered and should have been entered as 6042223. Notice how the lookup function returns the name Ronnie Smith instead of Lynn Murphy as the person called for 6042221. To prevent this error, edit the lookup function as follows: =vlookup(B15, phonenumbers, 2, false).

Adding the false argument to the lookup function causes it to return #N/A if a number not contained in the lookup table is entered.

8. Edit the lookup function for caller to prevent it from displaying the wrong caller when an incorrect telephone number is entered.

Table 8.12

	A	B	C
1	Number	Name	Friend of
2	8052961	Jennifer Lynch	Mary
3	2076693	Colm Anderson	Tony
4	3366011	Karen Flynn	Tony
5	5289945	Liam Davies	Linda
6	2896254	Kevin Barrett	Paul
7	7785543	Denis Carey	Linda
8	4045596	Niamh Carey	Linda
9	2518436	Mary Enright	Mary
10	3775049	Joan Leahy	Mary
11	6905431	Conor Kelly	Paul
12	6753026	Anne O Brien	Paul
13	6042223	Lynn Murphy	Paul
14	5196570	James O Rourke	Linda
15	3670259	Brian Walsh	Tony
16	5580169	Ronnie Smith	Mary

9. Format all money amounts to currency.

10. Use conditional formatting to highlight amounts over €1.00.

11. Delete all unused worksheets in the workbook.

12. In the worksheet named Telephone List implement spreadsheet protection so that data cannot be entered in any cells.

13. In the worksheet named Telephone Bill implement spreadsheet protection so that data can only be entered in the ranges A4:B28 and E4:E28. Formulas and functions shouldn't be displayed in the formula bar.

14. Save the spreadsheet as **Telephone Bill Analysis**.

 Tip: The first cell reference contained within a lookup function never refers to the lookup table. The lookup table should only be referred to in section two and section three of the lookup function.

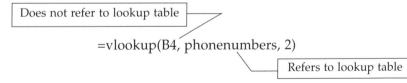

Does not refer to lookup table

=vlookup(B4, phonenumbers, 2)

Refers to lookup table

Table 8.13

	A	B	C	D	E
1	Telephone Bill				
2					
3	Date	Number	Person Called	Caller	Amount
4	01/07/2003	5196570			0.0950
5	03/07/2003	3670259			0.7767
6	03/07/2003	8052961			0.2848
7	06/07/2003	4045596			0.0950
8	08/07/2003	6905431			0.1126
9	08/07/2003	2076693			0.5129
10	10/07/2003	5196570			0.4857
11	12/07/2003	8052961			1.5851
12	15/07/2003	6753026			0.0950
13	23/07/2003	7785543			0.3352
14	28/07/2003	3775049			0.1293
15	04/08/2003	**6042221**			0.0950
16	08/08/2003	4045596			0.2187
17	08/08/2003	6042223			0.0950
18	11/08/2003	5580169			0.3157
19	15/08/2003	6042223			0.8857
20	16/08/2003	6905431			0.5560
21	20/08/2003	2518436			1.0222
22	22/08/2003	3775049			0.1419
23	23/08/2003	6753026			1.0264
24	27/08/2003	6905431			0.0950
25	27/08/2003	3775049			0.0950
26	27/08/2003	8052961			0.0950
27	29/08/2003	2896254			0.1213
28	30/08/2003	2518436			0.0950

Lookup Functions Assignment Two

1. Create a new spreadsheet workbook and rename Sheet1 as Tile Details.

2. Enter the data shown in Table 8.14 in the worksheet named Tile Details.

Table 8.14

	A	B	C	D	E	F	G
1	Product Code	Manufacturer	Tile Name	Colour	Height (metres)	Width (metres)	Unit Price
2	1	Tiles International	Fleurette	Navy	0.1	0.1	0.85
3	2	Tile Designs	Malibu	Light Blue	0.5	0.5	3.50
4	3	Tiles International	Textile	Light Brown	0.2	0.2	1.20
5	4	Northern Tiles	Florence	Purple	0.1	0.1	0.85
6	5	Northern Tiles	Paisley	Mixed	0.05	0.05	0.27
7	6	Tiles International	Serenity	Green	0.5	0.5	3.50
8	7	Tiles International	Opal	Indigo	0.1	0.1	0.90
9	8	Tile Designs	Marble	Grey	0.1	0.1	0.85
10	9	Tile Designs	Stone	Charcoal	0.2	0.2	1.15
11	10	Northern Tiles	Stone	Grey	0.1	0.1	0.80

3. Assign the name **tiles** to an appropriate range of cells.
4. Format unit prices to currency.
5. Rename Sheet2 as Customer Requirements.
6. Enter the data shown in Table 8.15 on page 172 in the worksheet named Customer Requirements. Formulas and functions will be entered in the shaded cells.
7. Create lookup functions to display the manufacturer, tile name, colour, height (metres) and width (metres) for each product code entered.
8. Calculate tile area (sq. metres).
9. Calculate the number of tiles required. (**Note:** Format this cell to zero decimal places to round the value up to the next whole number, as the tile shop doesn't sell parts of tiles.)[1]
10. Display unit price using a lookup function.
11. Calculate the total.
12. Rename Sheet3 as Sales Analysis.

---

[1] Values can also be rounded up using the Round function.

Table 8.15

	A	B	C	D	E	F	G	H	I	J	K	L
1	Customer	Product Code	Manufacturer	Tile Name	Colour	Height (metres)	Width (metres)	Tile Area (sq. metres)	Area to Cover (sq. metres)	No. of Tiles Required	Unit Price	Total
2	Paul O Shea	8							5.4			
3	Bob Finnegan	2							7.2			
4	Catherine Whelan	10							6.0			
5	Regina Irwin	3							10.5			
6	Ger Mullins	2							8.5			
7	Roy Byrne	5							2.5			
8	Matt Evans	8							4.1			
9	Betty Moore	9							4.9			
10	Maura Quinn	10							7.8			
11	Pat Whelan	1							6.5			
12	Kay Gallagher	5							1.6			
13	Diarmuid O Neill	7							8.2			
14	Mark Winters	3							10.6			

13. Enter the data displayed in Table 8.16 in the worksheet named Sales Analysis.

Table 8.16

	A	B	C
1	Manufacturer	Number of Tiles Sold	Sales Revenue
2	Tiles International		
3	Tile Designs		
4	Northern Tiles		

14. Calculate the total number of tiles sold by each manufacturer. Display totals without decimal places.

15. Calculate the total sales revenue for each manufacturer.

16. Display the number of tiles sold by each manufacturer using a pie chart with values displayed for each slice of the pie chart. The chart title is Units Sold by Manufacturer. Display the pie chart on the same worksheet as the data.

17. Display the total sales revenue by manufacturer using a pie chart with values displayed for each slice of the pie chart. The chart title is Sales Revenue by Manufacturer. Display the pie chart on the same worksheet as the data.

18. Delete all unused worksheets in the workbook.

19. Rearrange the sheet tabs so that they appear in the order shown in Figure 8.3.

\Customer Requirements / Tile Details / Sales Analysis /

Figure 8.3

20. In the Tile Details and Sales Analysis worksheets implement spreadsheet protection so that data cannot be entered in any cells.

21. In the Customer Requirements worksheet implement spreadsheet protection so that data can only be entered in the ranges A2:B14 and I2:I14. Formulas and functions shouldn't be displayed in the formula bar.

22. Protect the workbook for structure and windows.

23. Print the Customer Requirements and Sales Analysis worksheets.

24. Save the spreadsheet as **Tile Store**.

Lookup Functions Assignment Three

1. Create a new spreadsheet workbook and rename Sheet1 as List of PCs.

2. Enter the data shown in Table 8.17 on page 174 in the worksheet named List of PCs.

3. Assign the name **computers** to an appropriate range of cells.

4. Rename Sheet2 as Spare Parts.

5. Enter the data shown in Table 8.18 on page 175 in the worksheet named Spare Parts.

6. Assign the name **pcparts** to an appropriate range of cells.

Table 8.17

	A	B	C	D
1	PC Number	Model	Year of Purchase	Location
2	1	Dell Optiplex	1998	Marketing
3	2	Sony Vaio	2003	Marketing
4	3	Compaq Presario 6000	1999	Sales
5	4	Compaq Presario 8000	2003	Finance
6	5	Dell Inspiron 4100	2002	Engineering
7	6	Dell Optiplex	1999	Accounts
8	7	Compaq Presario 8000	2003	Administration
9	8	Dell Dimension	1998	Accounts
10	9	Compaq Presario 6000	2000	Human Resources
11	10	Dell Inspiron 4100	2003	Engineering
12	11	Dell Optiplex	2002	Sales
13	12	Sony Vaio	2003	Finance
14	13	Dell Dimension	1998	Engineering
15	14	Compaq Presario 6000	1998	Accounts
16	15	Dell Inspiron 4100	1999	Human Resources

7. Format all costs to currency.

8. Rename Sheet3 as Job Sheet.

9. Enter the data shown in Table 8.19 on page 176 in the worksheet named Job Sheet. Formulas and functions will be entered in the shaded cells.

10. Create lookup functions to display the model, year purchased and location for each PC number entered.

11. Create lookup functions to display the description and price for each part number entered.

12. Format all prices to currency.

13. Rename Sheet4 as Job Analysis.

14. Enter the data shown in Table 8.20 on page 177 in the worksheet named Job Analysis.

15. Calculate the total number of referrals made by each department.

16. Calculate the total cost of repairs for each department.

17. Display the number of referrals by department using a pie chart with percentages displayed for each slice of the pie chart. The chart title is Referrals by Department. Display the pie chart on the same worksheet as the data.

18. Display the total cost by department using a pie chart with values displayed for each slice of the pie chart. The chart title is Total Cost by Department. Display the pie chart on the same worksheet as the data.

Table 8.18

	A	B	C
1	Part No	Description	Cost
2	1	Mouse	13.97
3	2	3.5" Disk Drive	25.62
4	3	10 Gb Hard Disk	149.17
5	4	20 Gb Hard Disk	200.17
6	5	40 Gb Hard Disk	302.45
7	6	1.0 GHz Motherboard	335.13
8	7	1.5 GHz Motherboard	459.54
9	8	15" Monitor	183.35
10	9	17" Monitor	330.22
11	10	Telephone Cable	2.55
12	11	Modem	52.85
13	12	Keyboard	12.75
14	13	CD ROM Drive	40.16
15	14	DVD Drive	60.25
16	15	Power Supply Unit	24.37
17	16	Sound Card	32.17
18	17	Cat5 Cable	8.55
19	18	Network Card	25.00

19. Delete all unused worksheets in the workbook.
20. Rearrange the sheet tabs so that they appear in the order shown in Figure 8.4.

\ **Job Sheet** / List of PCs / Spare Parts / Job Analysis /

Figure 8.4

21. In the List of PCs, Spare Parts and Job Analysis worksheets implement spreadsheet protection so that data cannot be entered in any cells.
22. In the worksheet named Job Sheet implement spreadsheet protection so that data can only be entered in the ranges A4:A21 and E4:G21. Formulas and functions shouldn't be displayed in the formula bar.

Table 8.19

	A	B	C	D	E	F	G	H	I
1	PC Repair Workshop								
2									
3	PC Number	Model	Year Purchased	Location	Problem Description	Date Referred	Part No Used	Description	Price
4	13				Faulty mouse	02/07/2003	1		
5	1				Broken monitor	04/07/2003	8		
6	7				Not starting up	07/07/2003	6		
7	10				Failed hard drive	10/07/2003	5		
8	14				Won't connect to Internet	10/07/2003	10		
9	3				Keyboard stuck	14/07/2003	11		
10	1				Can't install new software	18/07/2003	12		
11	8				Won't connect to network	23/07/2003	17		
12	2				Mouse pointer jumping	25/07/2003	1		
13	13				Blank screen	29/07/2003	9		
14	2				Not powering up	01/08/2003	15		
15	10				Crashes frequently	06/08/2003	7		
16	14				Can't access files	08/08/2003	3		
17	7				Won't connect to network	08/08/2003	18		
18	4				Sound not working	13/08/2003	16		
19	1				Can't access files	18/08/2003	5		
20	3				Not powering up	21/08/2003	6		
21	10				Won't connect to Internet	29/08/2003	10		

Table 8.20

	A	B	C
1	Department	Number of Referrals	Total Cost
2	Accounts		
3	Administration		
4	Engineering		
5	Finance		
6	Marketing		
7	Sales		

23. Protect the workbook for structure and windows.
24. Save the spreadsheet as **PC Repair Workshop**.

9

Pivot Tables

In Chapter 9, you will learn how to

- Analyse data using a pivot table
- Create a pivot table report
- Create a pivot chart.

What is a Pivot Table?

Pivot tables can be used to analyse data when the same item occurs a number of times in a particular column.

Table 9.1

	A	B	C	D
1	College Expenditure			
2				
3	Month	Category	Amount	Teacher
4	May	Stationery	€57.32	John Mc Bride
5	May	Books	€105.90	Darina O Keefe
6	May	Software	€220.00	John Mc Bride
7	May	Stationery	€23.70	Noreen Walsh
8	May	Stationery	€45.68	Darina O Keefe
9	June	Hardware	€500.00	Mike Flynn
10	June	Books	€82.30	John Mc Bride
11	June	Software	€190.00	Mike Flynn
12	June	Books	€55.67	Noreen Walsh
13	June	Hardware	€1,090.00	Mike Flynn
14	June	Stationery	€120.43	Darina O Keefe
15	June	Stationery	€98.51	John Mc Bride

A pivot table can summarise data where items appear a number of times in a list

For example, in the spreadsheet displayed in Table 9.1, there are three purchases of books. The total amount spent on books can be calculated by adding the amounts for the three purchases, giving €243.87. Calculating totals for each category item would be very time consuming. A pivot table can do this instantly. A pivot table based on items in the category column would look something like Table 9.2.

Table 9.2

Category	Amount
Books	€243.87
Hardware	€1590.00
Software	€410.00
Stationary	€345.64

If we look at the teacher column we can see that each teacher's name is repeated a number of times. A pivot table could be used to calculate the total amount spent by each teacher, as follows in Table 9.3.

Table 9.3

Teacher	Amount
Darina O Keefe	€272.01
John Mc Bride	€458.13
Mike Flynn	€1780.00
Noreen Walsh	€79.37

Finally, if we look at the month column we can see that both May and June are repeated a number of times. A pivot table could be used to total the amount spent in each month, as follows in Table 9.4.

Table 9.4

Month	Amount
May	€452.60
June	€2136.91

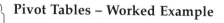

Pivot Tables – Worked Example

Create a new spreadsheet workbook and rename Sheet1 as Purchases. Enter the data shown in Table 9.5 on page 180 in the Purchases worksheet and format amounts to currency.

Table 9.5

	A	B	C	D
1	College Expenditure			
2				
3	Month	Category	Amount	Teacher
4	May	Stationery	57.32	John Mc Bride
5	May	Books	105.90	Darina O Keefe
6	May	Software	220.00	John Mc Bride
7	May	Stationery	23.70	Noreen Walsh
8	May	Stationery	45.68	Darina O Keefe
9	June	Hardware	500.00	Mike Flynn
10	June	Books	82.30	John Mc Bride
11	June	Software	190.00	Mike Flynn
12	June	Books	55.67	Noreen Walsh
13	June	Hardware	1,090.00	Mike Flynn
14	June	Stationery	120.43	Darina O Keefe
15	June	Stationery	98.51	John Mc Bride

We'll create pivot tables to analyse the total amount spent on each category, the total amount spent by each teacher and the total expenditure in each month.

1. Select **Data** followed by **Pivot Table** and **PivotChart** Report from the menu. Select 'Microsoft Excel list or database' as the data that you want to analyse and PivotTable as the type of report and then click Next, as shown in Figure 9.1 on page 181.
2. Highlight the data you want to use for the pivot table. Start from A3 to include the headings. Highlight A3:D30. Click Next, as shown in Figure 9.2 on page 181.

 Tip: It's a good idea to highlight additional blank rows to allow for data to be added as more purchases are made.

3. Excel now asks whether you want the pivot table on the same worksheet as the data or in a new worksheet. Select 'Existing worksheet' and click F3 to indicate the starting position for the pivot table as shown in Figure 9.3 on page 181. We must now specify the layout of the pivot table. Click the Layout button to display the Layout dialog box.

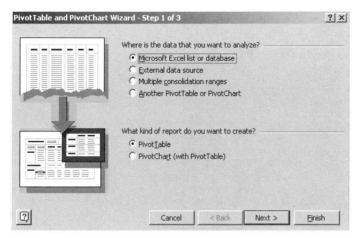

Figure 9.1

Figure 9.2

Figure 9.3

4. Drag Category and drop it in the ROW section, as shown in Figure 9.4 on page 182. Drag Amount and drop it in the DATA section. It changes to Sum of Amount, indicating that totals will be calculated for each category.

 Tip: If Count of Amount is displayed instead of Sum of Amount the wizard won't calculate the total. Double click Count of Amount and then select Sum from the 'Summarize by' list. In most cases, numeric fields are placed in the DATA section. Excel will normally calculate totals for each numeric field placed in the DATA section but can also calculate count, average, max and min. If a text field is placed in the DATA section, Excel will count the number of times each value in that field occurs in the pivot table range.

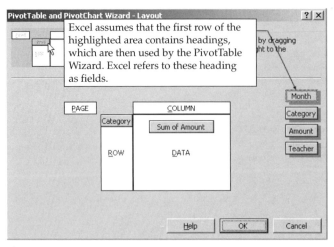

Figure 9.4

5. Click OK and then click Finish. The pivot table is displayed as follows in Figure 9.5.

Sum of Amount	
Category ▼	Total
Books	243.87
Hardware	1590
Software	410
Stationary	345.64
(blank)	
Grand Total	2589.51

Figure 9.5

Totals have been calculated for each category. An additional (blank) category has been added because we included blank rows in the pivot table range. As explained previously, including blank rows in the pivot table range means the pivot table can pick up additional data added later on.

6. To remove blank rows from the pivot table, click the downward pointing arrow to the right of Category to display the Categories, as shown in Figure 9.6.

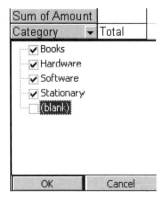

Figure 9.6

7. Remove the tick from the (blank) checkbox, as shown in Figure 9.6, and then click OK. Save the spreadsheet as **College Spending**.

Excel refers to each column heading as a field. In the College Spending spreadsheet the fields are Month, Category, Amount and Teacher. We can include some or all of these fields in each pivot table. The layout of the pivot table is determined by where the fields are placed, as shown in Figure 9.7.

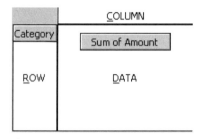

Figure 9.7

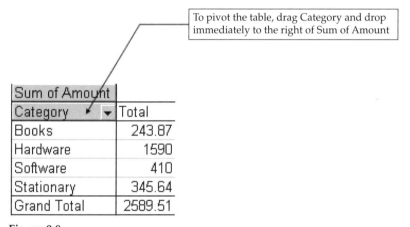

Figure 9.8

In the example shown in Figure 9.8, because category was placed in the ROW section, each category is displayed in a separate row on the extreme left of the pivot table. If category was placed in COLUMN instead of ROW as follows in Figure 9.9, then the pivot table would look like Figure 9.10 on page 184. Thus, a pivot table allows you to view your data in different ways.

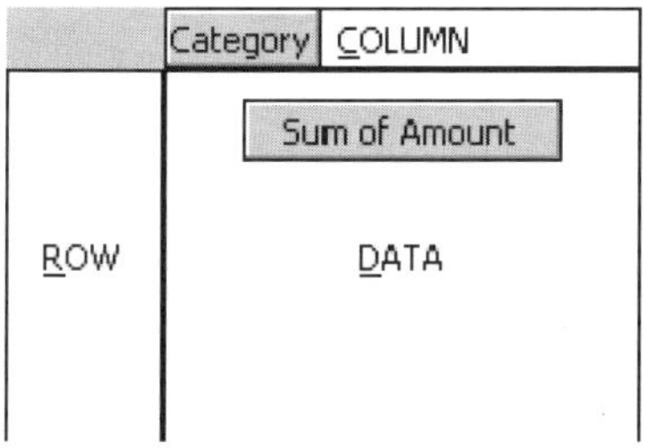

Figure 9.9

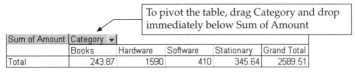

To pivot the table, drag Category and drop immediately below Sum of Amount

Sum of Amount	Category ▼				
	Books	Hardware	Software	Stationary	Grand Total
Total	243.87	1590	410	345.64	2589.51

Figure 9.10

Tip: Excel won't create a pivot table unless a field has been placed in the DATA section.

Formatting a Pivot Table

Format Report button

Figure 9.11

1. Open the College Spending spreadsheet if it isn't already open.
2. With the cell pointer in any cell in the pivot table, click the Format Report button in the pivot table toolbar.
3. Select Report 6 and click OK. Highlight the numbers contained within the pivot table and click the currency button (adjust column width if necessary).

Tip: If the pivot table toolbar isn't displayed, select **view** followed by **toolbars** from the menu. Now select pivot table from the list of toolbars.

Adding Data to a Pivot Table

As teachers make additional purchases during the year, this must be reflected in the pivot table. For example, if one of the teachers purchased additional books, the total for books should increase in the pivot table.

Add data to row 16 of the Purchases worksheet, as shown in Table 9.6.

Table 9.6

	A	B	C	D
16	June	Books	85.55	Noreen Walsh

The pivot table doesn't adjust automatically when new data is added – it must be refreshed. To refresh the pivot table, select any cell inside the pivot table and then click the Refresh Data button, as shown in Figure 9.12. The total for books then increases to €329.42 and the grand total increases to €2675.06.

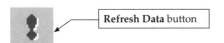

Refresh Data button

Figure 9.12

Creating a Pivot Table to Analyse the Total Spent by Each Teacher

1. Open the College Spending spreadsheet if it isn't already open.

2. Before creating the pivot table ensure that the cell pointer is in a blank cell and not in the existing pivot table.

PivotTable Wizard button

Figure 9.13

3. Click the PivotTable Wizard button or select Data, followed by PivotTable and PivotChart Report from the menu.

4. Select Microsoft Excel list or database as the data that you want to analyse and PivotTable as the type of report and then click Next.

5. Highlight A3:D30 as the data to be used in the pivot table and then click Next.

6. Excel now asks if you want to use less memory by basing this pivot table on the one you created earlier on. Click Yes. Your existing pivot table is highlighted. Click Next to go to the next step.

7. Select Existing Worksheet and click I3 as the starting cell of the pivot table.

8. Click the Layout button and set up your pivot table as follows in Figure 9.14.

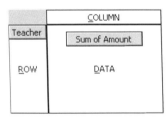

Figure 9.14

9. Click OK and then click Finish.

10. Remove the (blank) category from the pivot table.

11. With the cell pointer in any cell in the pivot table, click the Format Report button in the pivot table toolbar.

12. Select Report 6 and click OK. Highlight the numbers contained within the pivot table and click the currency button (adjust column width if necessary).

Pivot Tables Assignment One

1. Open the College Spending spreadsheet if it isn't already open.

2. Starting with the cell pointer in any cell outside an existing pivot table, create a pivot table linked to the range A3:D30. (When Excel asks if you want to base the pivot table on an existing one, click Yes and select any of the two pivot tables already created.)

3. Display the pivot table in the existing (Purchases) worksheet, starting at cell F12.

4. The pivot table should display the total amount spent in each month.

5. Remove the (blank) category from the pivot table.

6. Format the pivot table using Report 6 format and display the totals in currency format (check your answers: the total for May is €452.60. The total for June is €2,222.46).

7. Add data to row 17 of the Purchases worksheet, as shown in Table 9.7.

Table 9.7

	A	B	C	D
17	July	Stationary	52.67	Noreen Walsh

8. Click in any of the three pivot tables and then click the Refresh Data button to update all three pivot tables. Adding one additional row of data results in four changes in the pivot tables: the grand total increases to €2727.73, the total for stationery increases to €398.31, the total for Noreen Walsh increases to €217.59 and a new total of €52.67 is added for July. Updating all of these totals without a pivot table would be both time consuming and prone to error.

More Advanced Pivot Tables

Each of the three pivot tables that we created was based on two fields: category and amount, teacher and amount and month and amount. Adding more than two fields to a pivot table allows us to display data with a greater level of detail.

Creating a Pivot Table to Show the Total Amount Spent by Each Teacher on Each Category – Worked Example

1. Open the College Spending spreadsheet if it isn't already open.

2. Starting with the cell pointer in any cell outside an existing pivot table, create a pivot table linked to the range A3:D30. (When Excel asks if you want to base the pivot table on an existing one, click Yes and select any of the pivot tables already created.)

3. Select New Worksheet as the location of the pivot table.

4. This pivot table will break down the total amount spent by each teacher into categories. Click the Layout button and set up the pivot table as follows in Figure 9.15.

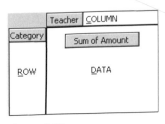

Figure 9.15

5. Click OK and then Finish. Remove (blank) from both teacher and category.

6. Format all numbers to currency.

7. Rename the worksheet that stores the pivot table as Expenditure by Category. The pivot table appears as follows in Figure 9.16.

Sum of Amount	Teacher								
Category	Darina O Keefe		John Mc Bride		Mike Flynn		Noreen Walsh		Grand Total
Books	€	105.90	€	82.30			€	141.22	€ 329.42
Hardware					€	1,590.00			€ 1,590.00
Software			€	220.00	€	190.00			€ 410.00
Stationary	€	166.11	€	155.83			€	76.37	€ 398.31
Grand Total	€	272.01	€	458.13	€	1,780.00	€	217.59	€ 2,727.73

Figure 9.16

Because teacher was placed in COLUMN there's a separate column for each teacher. Because category was placed in ROW there's a separate row for each category. Amounts are displayed where a teacher has spent money on a particular category.

8. Select any cell in the pivot table and then click the Format Report button. Select Report 6 and click OK. Highlight amounts and click the currency button. Increase column width if necessary. The pivot table is now displayed as follows in Figure 9.17.

Teacher	Category	Amount
Darina O Keefe		**€ 272.01**
	Books	€ 105.90
	Stationary	€ 166.11
John Mc Bride		**€ 458.13**
	Books	€ 82.30
	Software	€ 220.00
	Stationary	€ 155.83
Mike Flynn		**€ 1,780.00**
	Hardware	€ 1,590.00
	Software	€ 190.00
Noreen Walsh		**€ 217.59**
	Books	€ 141.22
	Stationary	€ 76.37
Grand Total		**€2,727.73**

Figure 9.17

Excel has formatted the data but it has also rearranged the order of the fields in the pivot table layout, as shown in Figure 9.18 and 9.19 on page 188.

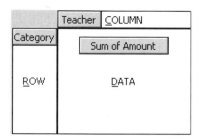

Figure 9.18 Original layout (before formatting)

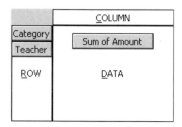

Figure 9.19 New layout (after formatting)

The ability to view the same data in different ways is a major advantage of pivot tables. Each time you create a pivot table it's a good idea to experiment with different layouts until you find the one that gets the message across most effectively. You can view the layout of your pivot table by right clicking any cell in the pivot table and then selecting Wizard, followed by Layout.

 Pivot Tables Assignment Two

1. Open the College Spending spreadsheet if it isn't already open.
2. Starting with the cell pointer in any cell outside an existing pivot table, create a pivot table linked to the range A3:D30 in the Purchases worksheet. Select New Worksheet as the location of the pivot table.
3. Click the Layout button and set up the pivot table as follows in Figure 9.20.

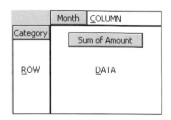

Figure 9.20

4. Remove (blank) from both Month and Category.
5. Rename the worksheet as Monthly Expenditure.
6. Format the pivot table using Report 6 and display Amounts in currency format.

7. Add data to row 18 of the Purchases worksheet, as shown in Table 9.8.

Table 9.8

	A	B	C	D
18	July	Staff Training	350.00	Darina O Keefe

8. Click in any of the five pivot tables and then click the Refresh Data button to update all five pivot tables. The Grand Total increases to €3,077.73 in all pivot tables. The total for Darina O Keefe increases to €622.01, the total for July becomes €402.67 and the Staff Training category is added to three of the pivot tables.
9. Click the Save button to save the changes.

Generating a Chart from a Pivot Table

To create a chart based on the data contained in the pivot table, simply click any cell in the pivot table and then click the Chart Wizard button. Excel creates a Column Chart on a new chart sheet. If you want to change the chart type and the chart titles click the Chart Wizard button again to display the Chart Wizard.

 Pivot Tables Assignment Three

1. Open the College Spending spreadsheet if it isn't already open.
2. In the worksheet named Expenditure by Category, select any cell in the pivot table.
3. In the Pivot Table toolbar click the Chart Wizard button.

 Chart Wizard button

Figure 9.21

4. Click the Chart Wizard button once more to display the Chart Wizard. Click Next and then change the chart title to Total Expenditure.
5. Click Next and with the 'Place chart as new sheet' option selected, enter Expenditure by Category Chart as the name for the new chart sheet.
6. In the worksheet named Monthly Expenditure select any cell in the pivot table.
7. In the PivotTable toolbar click the Chart Wizard button.
8. Click the Chart Wizard button once more to display the Chart Wizard. Click Next and then change the chart title to Total Expenditure.
9. Display the chart on a separate chart sheet named Monthly Expenditure Chart.

10. Add data to row 19 of the Purchases worksheet, as shown in Table 9.9.

Table 9.9

	A	B	C	D
19	July	Staff Training	350.00	John Mc Bride

11. Click in any pivot table and then click the Refresh Data button. The grand total in all pivot tables changes to €3427.73. A new column representing staff training has been added for John McBride in the Expenditure by Category Chart. In the Total Expenditure Chart, displayed in Figure 9.22, the staff training column has increased from €350 to €700.

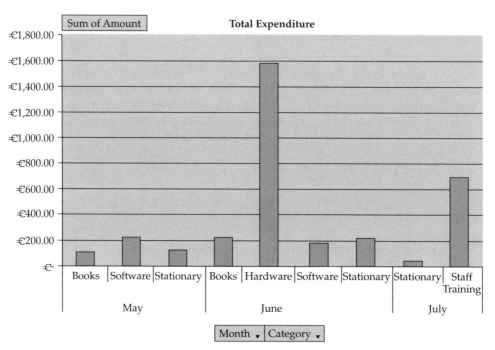

Figure 9.22

12. Click the Save button to save the changes.

Pivot Tables Assignment Four

Create a new spreadsheet workbook and rename Sheet1 as Flight Schedule. Enter the data displayed in Table 9.10 on page 191 in the Flight Schedule worksheet.

1. Create a pivot table in the Flight Schedule worksheet starting at cell G1, as displayed in Figure 9.23 on page 191.

Table 9.10

	A	B	C	D	E
1	Airline	Day	Time	Destination	Passengers
2	Aer Lingus	Monday	07:20	London	120
3	Ryanair	Monday	07:30	Manchester	75
4	Ryanair	Monday	08:00	London	140
5	Aer Lingus	Monday	08:45	Bristol	80
6	Aer Lingus	Monday	09:00	Manchester	120
7	Ryanair	Monday	09:30	Glasgow	85
8	Aer Lingus	Monday	10:00	London	100
9	Ryanair	Monday	10:30	London	120
10	Ryanair	Monday	10:45	Manchester	100
11	Aer Lingus	Monday	11:00	Glasgow	93

Tip: When highlighting the pivot table range, highlight the range A1:E22 to allow for data to be added later on.

2. Remove the (blank) category from the pivot table and format the pivot table as shown in Figure 9.23.

Airline ▾	Passengers
Aer Lingus	513
Ryanair	520
Grand Total	1033

Figure 9.23

3. Create a second pivot table in a separate worksheet, as displayed in Figure 9.24.
4. Remove the (blank) category from destination and airline and format the pivot table as shown in Figure 9.24. Rename the worksheet as Passengers by Destination.

Passengers	Airline ▾		
Destination ▾	Aer Lingus	Ryanair	Grand Total
Bristol	80		80
Glasgow	93	85	178
London	220	260	480
Manchester	120	175	295
Grand Total	513	520	1033

Figure 9.24

5. Generate a column chart from the pivot table. The chart title is Analysis of Passenger Numbers. Display the chart on a separate chart sheet named Sales Chart.

6. Create a third pivot table in the Flight Schedule worksheet starting at cell G9, using the layout displayed in Figure 9.25. Placing Destination in the PAGE section means that destinations can be selected from a drop down menu, as displayed in Figure 9.26.

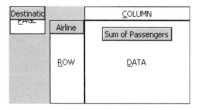

Figure 9.25

Destination	Manchester ▼
Airline ▼	**Passengers**
Aer Lingus	120
Ryanair	175
Grand Total	**295**

Figure 9.26

7. Remove the (blank) category from airline and format the pivot table by clicking the Format Report button.

8. View the passenger numbers on different routes by selecting destinations from the drop down menu.

9. Enter additional data starting at row 12 in the Flight Schedule worksheet, as shown in Table 9.11.

Table 9.11

	A	B	C	D	E
12	Aer Lingus	Tuesday	07:20	London	105
13	Ryanair	Tuesday	07:30	Manchester	89
14	Ryanair	Tuesday	08:00	London	140
15	Ryanair	Tuesday	08:30	Cork	55
16	Aer Lingus	Tuesday	08:45	Bristol	71
17	Aer Lingus	Tuesday	09:00	Manchester	109
18	Ryanair	Tuesday	09:30	Glasgow	100
19	Aer Lingus	Tuesday	10:00	London	105
20	Ryanair	Tuesday	10:30	London	119
21	Ryanair	Tuesday	10:45	Manchester	86
22	Aer Lingus	Tuesday	11:00	Glasgow	96

10. Refresh all pivot tables so that they include the new data (the new totals are 999 for Aer Lingus, 1109 for Ryanair and a grand total of 2108).

Tip: Make sure that the source of each pivot table includes cells in the range A1:E22.

11. Create a fourth pivot table in a separate worksheet, as displayed in Figure 9.27.

Airline	(All) ▼	
Destination ▼	**Day** ▼	**Passengers**
Bristol		**151**
	Monday	80
	Tuesday	71
Cork		**55**
	Tuesday	55
Glasgow		**374**
	Monday	178
	Tuesday	196
London		**949**
	Monday	480
	Tuesday	469
Manchester		**579**
	Monday	295
	Tuesday	284
Grand Total		**2108**

Figure 9.27

12. Rename the worksheet as Daily Passenger Numbers.
13. Delete all unused worksheets in the workbook.
14. Rearrange sheet tabs so that they are in the order shown in Figure 9.28.

Flight Schedule / Daily Passenger Numbers / Passengers by Destination / Sales Chart /

Figure 9.28

15. Print the Flight Schedule worksheet.
16. Save the spreadsheet as **Airline Destinations**.

Pivot Tables Assignment Five

1. Open the spreadsheet named Telephone Bill Analysis (created in Chapter 8: Lookup Functions).

2. Create a pivot table that analyses the telephone bill, as shown in Figure 9.29 on page 194. The pivot table should be on the same sheet as the data and should start at cell H3. (**Note:** *This is the total after changing the incorrectly entered phone number from 6042221 to 6042223.*)

Caller	▼	Amount
Linda		€ 1.23
Mary		€ 3.76
Paul		€ 3.08
Tony		€ 1.29
Grand Total		**€ 9.37**

Figure 9.29

3. Click the Save button to save the spreadsheet.

Toolbar Buttons Introduced in Chapter Nine

Figure 9.30   The **Format Report** button

With the cell pointer in any cell in a pivot table, click this button to see a selection of formats that can be applied to the pivot table. The format that you select will be applied to the entire pivot table.

Figure 9.31   The **Refresh Data** button

When the source data of the pivot table is edited, updated or added to, the pivot table doesn't update automatically. To see the effects of the changes on the pivot table, position the cell pointer in any cell in the pivot table and then click the Refresh Data button.

Figure 9.32   The **PivotTable Wizard** button

The PivotTable Toolbar is displayed once a pivot table has been created. Click the PivotTable Wizard button to create a new pivot table or to view the layout of an existing pivot table.

Figure 9.33   The **Chart Wizard** button

With the cell pointer in any cell in a pivot table, click this button to display the pivot table data with a column chart. Click the Chart Wizard button again to display the Chart Wizard where different chart types can be selected.

10

Spreadsheet Macros

 In Chapter 10, you will learn how to

- Automate repetitive tasks with macros
- Run macros from shortcut keys and command buttons
- Update data using Paste Special
- Develop a custom menu system using macros and command buttons.

 ## What are Macros?

Did you ever record yourself using a tape recorder? If you did, you would have started by pressing the record button and any sounds that were made were recorded until you pressed the stop button. When the tape is played back the sounds are recreated exactly as they occurred during recording.

A macro works in the same way, the only difference being that instead of recording and playing back sounds, a macro records and plays back spreadsheet tasks such as formatting and copying. When a macro is played back all the tasks that were recorded are carried out in an instant. This is where macros are really useful – they can greatly reduce the amount of time spent on mundane and repetitive spreadsheet tasks by automating tasks that are frequently carried out.

A word of warning about macros – they can contain viruses. When you open a spreadsheet that contains macros, Excel asks you whether you want to enable or disable macros. As long as you have created the macro yourself, it's safe to click the Enable button. On the other hand, if you've received an Excel workbook from an unknown source you should click the Disable button. A macro virus can't be executed once the macro is disabled.

 ## Creating a Macro – Worked Example

In the following example we'll create a macro that will generate an invoice heading for a computer supplies company.

1. Create a new spreadsheet workbook.
2. To start recording a new macro, select **Tools** followed by **Macro** from the menu.
3. Now select Record New Macro and enter invoiceheader as the name of the macro.

4. Enter the letter I as the shortcut key (this means that once the macro is recorded, it can be played back by holding down the CTRL key and typing i).

 Note: Excel will not allow you to include a space in a macro name.

5. Click OK to start recording the macro. The word 'Recording' appears at the bottom left of the screen.
 6. Type Computer Suppliers Ltd in cell A1 and press Enter.
 7. With the cell pointer in A1, increase the font size to 16.
 8. Highlight from A1 to J1 and then click the Merge and Centre button.
 9. Type Invoice in cell A2 and press Enter.
 10. With the cell pointer in A2, increase the font size to 14, click the bold button and change the font colour to blue.
 11. Highlight from A2 to J2 and then click the Merge and Centre button.
 12. Click the Stop Recording button if it's displayed. Alternatively, select Tools followed by Macro from the menu and then click Stop Recording.
 13. Save the spreadsheet as **Computer Invoice**. The spreadsheet should look something like Table 10.1.

Table 10.1

	A	B	C	D	E	F	G	H	I	J
1					**Computer Suppliers Ltd**					
2					Invoice					

Testing the Macro

1. Position the cell pointer in A1 of Sheet2.
 2. Hold down the CTRL key and type i.

When you play back a macro, all the steps carried out during recording are executed in one step at high speed. You can also play a macro by selecting **Tools** followed by **Macro** from the menu. Now click **Macros**, select the invoiceheader macro and click Run.
 The invoiceheader macro can be run in any other worksheet in the Computer Invoice spreadsheet. It can also be run in any other spreadsheet workbook as long as the Computer Invoice spreadsheet is open. Once the Computer Invoice spreadsheet is closed, the invoiceheader macro is not available to any other spreadsheet workbooks.

 Spreadsheet Macros Assignment One

1. Open the spreadsheet named Colour Predictor (created in Chapter 7).
 2. Record a new macro named erasecolours that performs the following tasks:
   • deletes the contents of B3

• deletes the contents of B5
• positions the cell pointer in B3.

3. Test the macro by entering different colour combinations and then running the macro.

4. Click the Save button to save the spreadsheet.

Tip: Holding down ALT and pressing the F8 key displays a list of all macros in the workbook.

Running a Macro from from a Button

Rather than running a macro either by selecting Tools followed by Macro from the menu or by holding down ALT, pressing F8 and selecting the required macro, it's much more efficient to link a macro to a button. The macro is then executed each time the button is clicked.

1. Open the Colour Predictor spreadsheet if it isn't already open.
2. Select **View** followed by **Toolbars** and then click **Forms** to display the Forms toolbar.

Note: You'll have to unprotect the worksheet first.

3. Click the Button button.

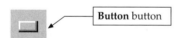

Figure 10.1

4. To the right of the Colour Predictor text, click and drag to draw a button.
5. The Assign Macro dialog box is displayed. Select erasecolours as the macro to run when the button is clicked and then click OK.
6. Highlight the text in the button (it will probably be something like 'Button 1') and type Clear. (***Note***: *Don't press Enter.*)
7. Click in any cell outside the button.
8. Re-protect the worksheet.
9. Close the Forms toolbar.
10. Click the Save button to save the spreadsheet. The result should look something like Figure 10.2.

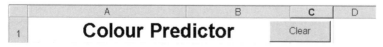

Figure 10.2

11. Test the macro by entering different colour combinations and then clicking the button.

Spreadsheet Macros Assignment Two

1. Open the spreadsheet named Ticket Sales Galway-Dublin Route (created in Chapter 3).

2. Record a new macro, named newweek, that performs the following tasks:

- Deletes the contents of B5:H9 in the worksheet named 0745
- Deletes the contents of B5:H9 in the worksheet named 1100
- Deletes the contents of B5:H9 in the worksheet named 1510
- Positions the cell pointer in B5 in the worksheet named 0745.

3. Using the Forms toolbar, draw a button to the right of the heading in the worksheet named 0745. Link this button to the newweek macro. The text for the button is 'Clear All'.

4. Test the macro by entering dummy ticket sales and then clicking the button.

Paste Special

We have already used cut and paste for moving data and copy and paste for copying data. When you select cut or copy the contents of the current cell or the highlighted range are placed in the clipboard, which is an area of temporary storage. Each time you select paste the contents of the clipboard are copied to the current worksheet, starting from the position of the cell pointer. If cells in the range that we pasted to already contain data, this data will be overwritten once paste is selected.

Paste Special allows us to copy data from a cell or range of cells and use this data to update data in another cell or range of cells.

Worked Example

1. Create a new spreadsheet workbook and rename Sheet1 as Stock. Enter the data shown in Table 10.2 on page 200.

2. Rename Sheet2 as Sales. Enter the data shown in Table 10.3 on page 200.

Data relating to units sold for each product in the Sales worksheet will be used to update the quantity in stock for each product in the Stock worksheet. For example, when we subtract the eight Crunchies sold from the 35 in stock, the new quantity in stock is 27.

Table 10.2

	A	B	C
1	Stock Levels		
2	Product Number	Product Name	Quantity in Stock
3	1	Crunchie	35
4	2	Snickers	20
5	3	Mars	23
6	4	Lion	15
7	5	Plain Chocolate	41
8	6	Rolo	12
9	7	Maltesers	28
10	8	Crisps	45

Table 10.3

	A	B	C
1	Sales		
2	Product Number	Product Name	Units Sold
3	1	Crunchie	8
4	2	Snickers	5
5	3	Mars	10
6	4	Lion	3
7	5	Plain Chocolate	12
8	6	Rolo	6
9	7	Maltesers	12
10	8	Crisps	26

Using Paste Special to Subtract Values

1. Highlight C3:C10, which is the range containing the units sold, in the Sales worksheet.
2. Click the Copy button on the toolbar.
3. Select cell C3 in the Stock worksheet.

4. Select **Edit** followed by **Paste Special** from the menu. The Paste Special dialog box is then displayed, as shown in Figure 10.3.

Figure 10.3

5. Select **Values** and **Subtract**, as shown in Figure 10.3, and then click OK. Values from the units sold column are subtracted from values in the quantity in stock column. The updated quantities in stock are displayed in Table 10.4.

Table 10.4

	A	B	C
1	Stock Levels		
2	Product Number	Product Name	Quantity in Stock
3	1	Crunchie	27
4	2	Snickers	15
5	3	Mars	13
6	4	Lion	12
7	5	Plain Chocolate	29
8	6	Rolo	6
9	7	Maltesers	16
10	8	Crisps	19

6. Rename Sheets3 as Purchases. Enter the data shown in Table 10.5 on page 202.

As new stock is purchased, this data is used to update the stock levels in the Stock worksheet. For example, when we add the 20 Crunchies sold to the 27 in stock, the new quantity in stock is 47.

Table 10.5

	A	B	C
1	Purchases		
2	Product Number	Product Name	Units Purchased
3	1	Crunchie	20
4	2	Snickers	10
5	3	Mars	25
6	4	Lion	15
7	5	Plain Chocolate	15
8	6	Rolo	15
9	7	Maltesers	25
10	8	Crisps	30

Using Paste Special to Add Values

1. Highlight C3:C10, which is the range containing the units purchased, in the Purchases worksheet.
2. Click the Copy button on the toolbar.
3. Select cell C3 in the Stock worksheet.
4. Select **Edit** followed by **Paste Special** from the menu. The Paste Special dialog box is then displayed.

Figure 10.4

5. Select **Values** and **Add**, as shown in Figure 10.4, and then click OK. Values from the units purchased column are added to the values in the quantity in stock column. The updated quantities in stock are displayed in Table 10.6 on page 203.
6. Save the spreadsheet as **Stock Control**.

Table 10.6

	A	B	C
1	Stock Levels		
2	Product Number	Product Name	Quantity in Stock
3	1	Crunchie	47
4	2	Snickers	25
5	3	Mars	38
6	4	Lion	27
7	5	Plain Chocolate	44
8	6	Rolo	21
9	7	Maltesers	41
10	8	Crisps	49

Bringing it all Together

In the following assignment you'll use macros, Paste Special, IF functions, lookup functions and sorting.

1. Create a new spreadsheet workbook and rename Sheet1 as Team Details.
2. Enter the data shown in Table 10.7 in the worksheet named Team Details.

Table 10.7

	A	B	C
1	Team Number	Team Name	Manager
2	1	Manchester United	Alex Ferguson
3	2	Liverpool	Gerard Houlier
4	3	Arsenal	Arsen Wenger
5	4	Leeds United	Terry Venables
6	5	Newcastle United	Bobby Robson
7	6	Chelsea	Claudio Ranieri

3. Assign the name teams to the range A2:C7.
4. Implement spreadsheet protection so that no data can be entered in this worksheet. (**Note:** *Don't enter a password when you protect the worksheet. This is important for the macro that we'll create later on.*)

5. Rename Sheet2 as League Table.

6. Enter the data shown in Table 10.8 in the worksheet named League Table. Formulas and functions are required in the shaded cells.

Table 10.8

	A	B	C	D	E	F	G
1	Team Number	Team Name	Goals For	Goals Against	Goal Difference	Total Points	Manager
2	1						
3	2						
4	3						
5	4						
6	5						
7	6						

7. Display the team name and manager for each team number using appropriate functions.

8. Insert a formula to calculate the goal difference (goals for minus goals against).

NOTE

Note: Data relating to goals for and against will be entered later on.

9. Implement spreadsheet protection so that data can only be entered in the ranges C2:D7 and F2:F7 and so that formulas and functions aren't displayed in the formula bar. (**Note:** *Don't enter a password when you protect the worksheet.*)

10. Rename Sheet3 as Fixtures.

11. Enter the data shown in Table 10.9 in the worksheet named Fixtures.

Table 10.9

	A	B	C	D	E	F	G	H	I
1	Team Number	Home Team		Team Number	Away Team	Home Team Goals	Away Team Goals	Home Team Points	Away Team Points
2	1		vs.	2		3	1		
3	3		vs.	4		2	2		
4	5		vs.	6		0	1		

12. In cell B2 enter a function that displays the team name corresponding to the team number entered in A2. Copy this function to B3 and B4.

13. In cell E2 enter a function that displays the team name corresponding to the team number entered in D2. Copy this function to E3 and E4.

14. In cell H2 enter a function that calculates the home team points (three points for a win, one point for a draw, zero points for losing). Enter a similar function in I2 to calculate the away team points. Copy these functions to rows three and four.

15. Implement spreadsheet protection so that data can only be entered in the ranges A2:A4, D2:D4 and F2:G4 and so that formulas and functions aren't displayed in the formula bar. (**Note:** *Don't enter a password when you protect the worksheet.*)

16. Rename Sheet4 as Points from Current Fixture.

17. Enter the following data shown in Table 10.10 in the worksheet named Points from Current Fixture.

Table 10.10

	A	B	C	D	E
1	Team Number	Team Name	Goals For	Goals Against	Total Points
2					
3					
4					
5					
6					
7					

The worksheet displayed in Table 10.10 will store and rearrange data from the worksheet named Fixtures. This data will be used to update the League Table worksheet. The data must be rearranged so that it has the same order and structure as the data in the League Table worksheet. When both worksheets have the same order and structure, Paste Special can be used to add goals for, goals against and total points from Points from the Current Fixture worksheet to the corresponding values in the League Table worksheet. Rearranging the order of the data requires linking formulas.

- **Linking formula one**: In A2, enter a formula that links to the team number stored in A2 in the worksheet named Fixtures. Copy this formula first to A3 and A4 and then to B2, B3 and B4.
- **Linking formula two**: In A5, enter a formula that links to the team number stored in D2 in the worksheet named Fixtures. Copy this formula first to A6 and A7 and then to B5, B6 and B7.
- **Linking formula three**: In C2, enter a formula that links to the home team goals stored in F2 in the worksheet named Fixtures. Copy this formula first to C3 and C4 and then to D2, D3 and D4.
- **Linking formula four**: In C5, enter a formula that links to the away team goals stored in G2 in the worksheet named Fixtures. Copy this formula to C6 and C7.
- **Linking formula five**: In D5, enter a formula, that links to the home team goals stored in F2 in the worksheet named Fixtures. Copy this formula to D6 and D7.

- **Linking formula six**: In E2, enter a formula that links to the home team points stored in H2 in the worksheet named Fixtures. Copy this formula to E3 and E4.
- **Linking formula seven**: In E5, enter a formula that links to the away team points in I2 in the worksheet named Fixtures. Copy this formula to E6 and E7.

18. Protect the worksheet so that no data can be entered and that formulas and functions aren't displayed in the toolbar. (**Note:** *Don't enter a password when you protect the worksheet.*)

19. Save the spreadsheet as **Football League**.

Updating the League Table worksheet with data from current fixtures is carried out in a number of steps. Each step requires a separate macro.

Macro One

The league table and points from current Fixture worksheets must be unprotected so that they can be sorted.

Create a macro named **unprotect**. The macro should carry out the following steps:

- Click the League Table sheet tab
- Unprotect the worksheet
- Click the Points from Current Fixture sheet tab
- Unprotect the worksheet.

 Tip: The first line of each macro, which selects the worksheet, is very important. Without it, the macro may be executed in the wrong worksheet at a later stage. You should click the sheet tab as the first step in each macro even if the correct worksheet is already displayed to ensure that this line of code is added to each macro.

Macro Two

The teams in the League Table worksheet must be sorted in ascending order of team number.

Create a macro named **sortleaguetablebyteamno**. The macro should carry out the following steps:

- Click the League Table sheet tab
- Select any cell containing a team number in column A
- Sort in ascending order.

Macro Three

The teams in the points from Current Fixture worksheet must be sorted in ascending order of team number (the sorts are required to ensure that the correct values from the points from Current Fixture worksheet are used to update each team's goals for, goals against and total points).

Create a macro named **sortpointsfromcurrentfixture**. The macro should carry out the following steps:

- Click the Points from Current Fixture sheet tab
- Select any cell containing a team number in column A
- Sort in ascending order.

Macro Four

Values for goals for, goals against and total points from the Points from Current Fixtures worksheet are used to update the corresponding values for all teams in the League Table worksheet using Paste Special, values and add.

Create a macro named **updateleaguepoints**. The macro should carry out the following steps:

- Click the Points from Current Fixture sheet tab
- Copy C2:D7 in Points from Current Fixture to C2:D7 in the League Table worksheet using Paste Special, values and add
- Copy E2:E7 in Points from Current Fixture to F2:F7 in the League Table worksheet using Paste Special, values and add.

Macro Five

The team numbers and goals for both home and away teams must be deleted from the Fixtures worksheet.

Create a macro named **clearfixtures**. The macro should carry out the following steps:

- Click the Fixtures sheet tab
- Delete the contents of A2:A4, D2:D4 and F2:G4.

Macro Six

The League Table worksheet must be sorted first in descending order of points and then in descending order of goal difference.

Create a macro named **sortleaguetablebypoints.** The macro should carry out the following steps:

- Click the League Table sheet tab
- Highlight A1:G7
- Sort in descending order of total points and then in descending order of goal difference.

Macro Seven

The League Table and Points from Current Fixture worksheets must be re-protected.
Create a macro named **reprotect**. The macro should carry out the following steps:

- Click the League Table sheet tab
- Protect the worksheet (don't enter a password)
- Click the Points from Current Fixture sheet tab
- Protect the worksheet (don't enter a password)

Macro Eight

Finally, the League Table worksheet must be selected to display the results.
Create a macro named **viewleague**. The macro should carry out the following steps:

- Click the League Table sheet tab
- Select cell A1.

Updating the League Table worksheet requires that each of the eight macros be executed in sequence. Running each macro individually would be tedious and time consuming so the solution is to create another macro that will run each of the eight macros in sequence. This time we have to write the macro ourselves using the Visual Basic editor.

1. Press ALT and F8 to list macros already created and then click Edit. The code for macros already created is displayed.
2. Press the down arrow on the keyboard until you get to the first blank line after the last macro.
3. Each macro starts with the word 'Sub', followed by the name of the macro and then followed by an opening and closing bracket. All macros end with the words 'End Sub'. Type Sub Update and press Enter. Excel adds opening and closing brackets after the name of the macro and inserts End Sub at the end of the macro. Your macro now appears as follows:

```
Sub Update ( )
End Sub
```

The commands executed by the macro are entered on separate lines between Sub and End Sub.
Type the commands displayed below.

```
Sub Update( )
    unprotect
    sortleaguetablebyteamno
    sortpointsfromcurrentfixture
    updateleaguepoints
```

```
    clearfixtures
    sortleaguetablebypoints
    reprotect
    viewleague
End Sub
```

4. Select the Football League spreadsheet in the taskbar and unprotect the Fixtures worksheet. Draw a command button and link it to the macro named Update. The text for the button is Update League Table. Re-protect the Fixtures worksheet.

Running the Macro

1. Before running the macro delete goals for, goals against and total points in the League Table worksheet. Delete all team numbers and both home and away goals in the Fixtures worksheet. Check that all worksheets are protected. Click the Save button to save the spreadsheet.

2. Enter the results displayed in Table 10.11 in the Fixtures worksheet.

3. Run the macro by clicking the Update League Table button in the Fixtures worksheet. The resulting League Table worksheet should look like Table 10.12 on page 210.

Table 10.11

	A	B	C	D	E	F	G
1	Team Number	Home Team		Team Number	Away Team	Home Team Goals	Away Team Goals
2	1		vs.	2		3	1
3	3		vs.	4		2	2
4	5		vs.	6		0	1

Creating a Menu System

1. Rename Sheet5 as Menu (insert a new worksheet if necessary).
2. Create macros nine and ten.

Macro Nine

Create a macro named **enterresults**. The macro should carry out the following steps:

- Select the worksheet named Fixtures
- Select cell A2.

Table 10.12

	A	B	C	D	E	F	G
1	Team Number	Team Name	Goals For	Goals Against	Goal Difference	Total Points	Manager
2	1	Manchester United	3	1	2	3	Alex Ferguson
3	6	Chelsea	1	0	1	3	Claudio Ranieri
4	3	Arsenal	2	2	0	1	Arsen Wenger
5	4	Leeds United	2	2	0	1	Terry Venables
6	5	Newcastle United	0	1	–1	0	Bobby Robson
7	2	Liverpool	1	3	–2	0	Gerard Houlier

Macro Ten

Create a macro named **displaymenu**. The macro should carry out the following steps:

- Select the worksheet named Menu
- Select cell A1.

3. Draw a command button in the Menu worksheet and link the button to the enterresults macro. The text for the button is Enter Results.

4. Draw a second command button in the Menu worksheet and link the button to the viewleague macro. The text for the button is View League.

5. Set up the Menu worksheet as displayed in Figure 10.5.

6. Unprotect the Fixtures worksheet, draw a command button in the Fixtures worksheet and link the button to the displaymenu macro. The text for the button is Exit. Re-protect the Fixtures worksheet (don't enter a password).

7. Unprotect the League Table worksheet. Draw a command button in the League Table worksheet and link the button to the displaymenu macro. The text for the button is Exit. Re-protect the League Table worksheet (don't enter a password).

Figure 10.5

8. With the cell pointer in any cell in the Menu worksheet, select **Tools** followed by **Options** from the menu. Remove the tick from the Sheet Tabs check box. This means the worksheet names will no longer be displayed on sheet tabs at the bottom of the screen.

9. Click the Enter Results button and enter the second round of fixtures, as shown in Table 10.13.

Table 10.13

	A	B	C	D	E	F	G
1	Team Number	Home Team		Team Number	Away Team	Home Team Goals	Away Team Goals
2	2		vs.	3		2	1
3	4		vs.	5		0	2
4	6		vs.	1		1	1

10. Click the Update League Table button.

11. Return to the menu, click the Enter Results button and enter the third round of fixtures, as shown in Table 10.14.

Table 10.14

	A	B	C	D	E	F	G
1	Team Number	Home Team		Team Number	Away Team	Home Team Goals	Away Team Goals
2	3		vs.	6		3	1
3	1		vs.	4		1	2
4	5		vs.	2		3	2

12. Click the Update League Table button.

13. Return to the menu, click the Enter Results button and enter the fourth round of fixtures, as shown in Table 10.15.

Table 10.15

	A	B	C	D	E	F	G
1	Team Number	Home Team		Team Number	Away Team	Home Team Goals	Away Team Goals
2	2		vs.	6		3	1
3	4		vs.	3		2	0
4	1		vs.	5		1	1

14. Click the Update League Table button.

15. Return to the menu, click the Enter Results button and enter the final round of fixtures, as shown in Table 10.16.

Table 10.16

	A	B	C	D	E	F	G
1	Team Number	Home Team		Team Number	Away Team	Home Team Goals	Away Team Goals
2	6		vs.	4		2	2
3	5		vs.	3		3	2
4	2		vs.	1		2	0

16. Click the Update League Table button. The final team positions should be as follows in the League Table worksheet shown in Table 10.17.

17. Click the Save button to save the spreadsheet.

Table 10.17

	A	B	C	D	E	F	G
1	Team Number	Team Name	Goals For	Goals Against	Goal Difference	Total Points	Manager
3	5	Newcastle United	9	6	3	10	Bobby Robson
3	2	Liverpool	10	8	2	9	Gerard Houlier
4	4	Leeds United	8	7	1	8	Terry Venables
5	1	Manchester United	6	7	−1	5	Alex Ferguson
6	6	Chelsea	6	9	−3	5	Claudio Ranieri
7	3	Arsenal	8	10	−2	4	Arsen Wenger

Independent Challenge

If you're feeling adventurous at this stage, try adding matches played, matches won, matches drawn and matches lost as four extra columns in the League Table worksheet. Amend worksheets and macros where necessary to include these statistics in the soccer league system.

Toolbar Buttons Introduced in Chapter Ten

This button is part of the Forms toolbar. Click the Button button and then draw a rectangle to create a button that runs a macro.

Figure 10.6 The **Button** button

Progress Test 2

Complete the test by writing answers in the space provided or by circling the correct answer.

1. By default, all cells in a spreadsheet workbook are:

a. Locked
b. Unlocked

2. Once a worksheet is protected data can only be entered in:

a. Locked cells
b. Unlocked cells

3. You entered your password to unprotect the worksheet and Excel displayed the message 'The password you supplied is not correct'. List two possible errors that would have caused this message to be displayed.

a. _____
b. _____

4. The spreadsheet displayed in Table 10.18 on page 214 calculates the cost of a package holiday. Assuming that formulas/functions have been entered in the range G2:J8:

a. Identify the range of cells that should be unlocked. _____
b. Identity the range of cells that should be hidden. _____
c. Once the worksheet is protected, which cells will the spreadsheet user have access to? _____
d. Identify two advantages of protecting this spreadsheet. _____
_____

5. The number of IFs required in a nested IF function is determined by:

a. The number of conditions
b. The number of actions

Table 10.18

	A	B	C	D	E	F	G	H	I	J
1	Client Name	Destination	Adults	Children	Depart Date	Return Date	Number of Nights	Price	Discount	Total
2	Alex Smith	Costa Brava	2	1	19/07/2003	02/08/2003	14	€850	€42	€808
3	Jo Keane	Ibiza	2	3	19/07/2003	02/08/2003	14	€1200	€180	€1020
4	Tim Whelan	Canaries	4	0	19/07/2003	26/08/2003	7	€1600	€0	€1600
5	Michelle Riordan	Ibiza	2	2	20/07/2003	03/08/2003	14	€900	€90	€810
6	Tony O Connor	Palermo	6	0	26/07/2003	09/08/2003	14	€2500	€0	€2500
7	Cathy Sheehan	Canaries	2	1	26/07/2003	09/08/2003	14	€1000	€50	€950
8	Andrea Connolly	Ibiza	2	4	27/07/2003	10/08/2003	14	€1150	€230	€920

6. Write down the name of each logical operator displayed in Table 10.19.

Table 10.19

Logical Operator	Meaning
=	
<	
<=	
>	
>=	
<>	

7. Which function can be used to test multiple conditions when all the conditions must be satisfied? _____

8. Identify the error in the IF function displayed below:

=if(and(B2>100,C2="Yes"),D2*5%)

9. When Excel displays a blue dot in a cell this indicates:

a. A bracket is missing from a function
b. Incorrect use of a logical operator in an IF function
c. A formula or function contains a circular reference
d. Incorrect use of an arithmetic operator in a formula

10. Indicate below the sections of an IF function where use of logical operators is not permitted.

a. Condition
b. True action
c. False action

11. Why will the following IF function return an error? =if(A2<18:00,0.6,0.2)
12. Which function is required to access data from Table 10.20? _____

Table 10.20

Item Number	1	2	3	4
Description	Appointments Book	Telephone Calls Book	Postages Book	Time Book
Price	€18.93	€14.66	€13.33	€9.56

13. A pivot table can't function unless a field is placed in the:

a. Page section
b. Row section
c. Column section
d. Data section

14. Once the source data of a pivot table changes, the effects of the changes can be seen in the pivot table by clicking which of the following buttons?

a.

Figure 10.7

b.

Figure 10.8

c.

Figure 10.9

d.

Figure 10.10

15. Which of the following toolbars is required to draw a button to run a macro?

a. Standard toolbar
b. Formatting toolbar
c. Drawing toolbar
d. Forms toolbar

16. Which key combination can be used to display macros in a workbook?

a. Shift + F2
b. ALT + F8
c. CTRL + F2
d. Shift + F8

SECTION 3

Project Guidelines and Sample Exams

11

Project Guidelines and Sample Exams

As part of the FETAC (NCVA) Level 2 Spreadsheet Methods Module you are required to complete a spreadsheet project. The project tests if you can apply what you have learned about spreadsheets to a fictitious problem and then design and create a spreadsheet to solve the problem. The problem may be in a business context, such as the need to computerise the payroll of a small business, or it may be in relation to an interest or hobby, such as the need to create a spreadsheet to maintain the league table of a local football league.

The spreadsheet project must be completed in three distinct phases.

1. Phase one: design (40%)
2. Phase two: implementation (40%)
3. Phase three: proposed modifications (20%).

The project must be completed in this order. You must design your spreadsheet on paper before you set it up in Excel. It's worth noting that there are more marks for designing your spreadsheet and for suggesting modifications than for creating the spreadsheet in Excel. Many students spend too much time on setting up the spreadsheet and not enough time on design and modifications.

Phase One – Design (40%)

1. Describe the aims of your project
2. Specify input and output data
3. Design a data capture form
4. Specify formulas and functions used for processing.

Describe the Aims of Your Project

1. Provide some background information to set the scene for your project.

Example

Widget Engineering Ltd. is a small engineering firm that employs 12 people. Payment of wages in the company is done weekly and is calculated using a manual payroll system. This system is very complicated and above all very time consuming. It's also prone to error.

The aim of this project is to computerise the payroll system using a spreadsheet. The new system will ensure that all calculations and weekly wages slips will be processed quickly and efficiently with the minimum amount of problems.

2. Identify problems that exist in the system you've decided to computerise using a spreadsheet. For each problem that you identify, describe in detail how the spreadsheet will solve the problem.

Example

Problem: With the manual system each employee's weekly tax and tax to date are worked out by the accounts clerk, using a calculator. As many of the employees work overtime, the amount of tax varies from week to week. Due to the number of calculations required, the clerk sometimes makes a mistake and is unavailable for other work while the wages are being calculated.

Solution: In the spreadsheet system, each employee's tax rate will be worked out using an IF function. The clerk will no longer have to work out when an employee moves onto the higher rate of tax because the spreadsheet will make this decision in the future. Tax to date will be automatically calculated by adding this week's tax onto the tax paid to date using a macro and Paste Special.

Specify Input and Output Data

1. Identify where the data that's going to be entered in your spreadsheet exists in the current system.

Example

RSI number: everyone is given an RSI number by the Tax Department. This is kept on record in each employee's file.

Rate per hour: each employee is on a different rate per hour. These are stored in the employee files in the personnel department.

2. Input and output data should be identified and should be specified using the following headings: Variable Name, Data Type, Format and Example. Input data is data that's entered in the spreadsheet, e.g. hours worked and rate per hour. Output data is data that's calculated using formulas or functions, e.g. weekly gross pay and weekly PAYE.

Input Data Example

Table 11.1

Variable Name	Data Type	Format	Example
Employee Name	Text	Arial, 14	Tom Jenkins
Annual Salary	Numeric	Currency, 0 decimals	€32,560

Output Data Example

Table 11.2

Variable Name	Data Type	Format	Example
Weekly Gross Pay	Numeric	Currency, 2 decimals	€626.15
Weekly PRSI	Numeric	Currency, 2 decimals	€21.92

3. Identify which areas of the spreadsheet are protected and can only be accessed by entering a password. The spreadsheet user should only have access to cells where data is inputted. All other cells should be protected. In some cases an entire worksheet, such as a worksheet containing a lookup table, may be hidden. Formulas should be hidden and should require a password in order to view them.

Design a Data Capture Form

A data capture form is a printed form that's used to collect data before it's entered in the spreadsheet. It should be designed to capture all the input data. We have all filled in data capture forms at one time or another: club membership forms, an application for a bank account or the CAO form. It's a good idea to look at how data capture forms are designed in practice before you create your own. A well-designed data capture form will:

- Be easy to complete
- Contain instructions on how to complete the form
- Indicate to whom the form is to be returned or where the form is to be sent when it's completed
- Be well laid out on the page using appropriate fonts, colours, tick boxes and lines (for writing names and addresses).

Specify Formulas and Functions Used for Processing

Example

Weekly gross pay = annual salary divided by 52.
PRSI = IF PRSI Code = "AO" or "AX" then gross pay for tax purposes is multiplied by 8.5%, otherwise gross pay for tax purposes is multiplied by 12%.

Phase Two – Implementation (40%)

1. Spreadsheet well designed
2. Cell formats appropriately applied

3. Formulas and functions accurately applied
4. Change of variable
5. Spreadsheets saved on disk and printouts.

Spreadsheet Well Designed

In general your spreadsheet will contain at least three worksheets, as follows.

1. One worksheet where the user will enter the input data. The layout of this worksheet should match the layout of the data capture form and both should include the same items of input data.
2. One worksheet that contains all the formulas and functions. This worksheet does the data processing.
3. One worksheet that displays the results of the data processing, e.g. a wages slip.

Depending on the nature of your project you may require more than three worksheets. If you're using a lookup table, this should be stored in a separate worksheet.

Cell Formats Appropriately Applied

- Headings and data should be aligned as appropriate.
- Correct formats should be used for currency, percentages and decimal places. The spreadsheet should be formatted in a way that makes it attractive and easy to use.
- Colour should be used appropriately. Use of a particular colour to identify cells where data is input often makes a spreadsheet easier to use.

Formulas and Functions Accurately Applied

- The spreadsheet should at least contain an IF function or a lookup function.
- The results of calculations performed by the spreadsheet should be correct. This should be tested by carrying out the same calculations on paper and checking to see if the results are the same as those produced by the spreadsheet.
- A printout of all formulas and functions contained in your spreadsheet must be produced (formulas and functions can be displayed by selecting **Tools** followed by **Options** and then clicking **Formulas**). Save this version of your spreadsheet workbook under a different name, such as Spreadsheet Project Formulas.

Change of Variable

If the worksheets are linked correctly, changing a numeric input data variable, e.g. hours worked, should cause data to change, e.g. gross pay, tax and net pay, in the output sheet. This must be demonstrated by changing an item of input data, printing this altered input sheet and also printing out the resulting output sheet. Save this version of the spreadsheet under a different name, such as Project Variable Change.

Spreadsheets Saved on Disk and Printouts

When you have completed the project you should have three versions of your spreadsheet saved on disk (each with a different name) and also a printout of each.

Table 11.3

Spreadsheets Saved on Disk	
Version	Example
Original spreadsheet workbook	Spreadsheet Project.xls
Spreadsheet with formulas and functions displayed	Spreadsheet Project Formulas.xls
Spreadsheet with input variable changed	Project Variable Change.xls

Phase Three – Proposed Modifications (20%)

Suggest at least three ways in which your spreadsheet could be improved if you had more time. Often as students are working on a project they notice limitations in the design of the spreadsheet. These should be noted and used as potential modifications. Because this section of the project is worth 20%, an in-depth description of each modification is required. Modifications should be illustrated using examples and diagrams where appropriate.

Example

At the moment Widget Engineering Ltd. employs 12 people. In the spreadsheet all of the formulas and functions are set up to handle the earnings of these 12 people.

In the event of a new employee joining the company, a new worksheet would have to be set up for them together with additional rows and columns being added to the processing sheet to do the wages calculations for the new employee. At the moment the set-up of the spreadsheet doesn't allow this to be done automatically. Either an existing worksheet would have to be copied and then amended or a completely new worksheet would have to be set up from scratch. Apart from this being very time consuming, it can be a difficult task for anyone who is unfamiliar with this system.

Given more time, I would create a macro to solve this problem. Each time the macro is run it would add a new worksheet to the spreadsheet and adjust the processing sheet to accommodate the new employee. The accounts clerk would no longer have to go through the painstaking process of setting up a new input sheet and creating new formulas and functions in the processing sheet, as this would be done automatically when the macro is run.

Possible Spreadsheet Project Topics

- **Foreign exchange**: Create a spreadsheet that converts amounts entered in euros to an equivalent amount for a selection of currencies outside the euro zone.
- **Home decoration estimates**: Set up a spreadsheet that will produce a quote for decorating a room where dimensions of the room can be entered and the type of paint and/or tiles can be selected from a list.
- **Travel allowances**: Produce a weekly travel expense report for sales reps who claim for mileage and overnight accommodation allowances.
- **Exam grades**: Create a spreadsheet that allows a teacher to enter student marks per subject and which will then produce a sorted report of students and grades.
- **Car rentals**: Create a spreadsheet that calculates the daily rental fee depending on the type of car. Special offers might be applied to off-peak times.
- **Fantasy football league**: Set up a spreadsheet that allocates points to teams in a league where the total points per game depend on the actions of each player in the team. For example, five points could be awarded to a player for scoring a goal.
- **Cash flow analysis**: Record the income and expenditure of a company over a twelve-month period using a spreadsheet. The spreadsheet should alert the user when creditors must be paid or when customer payments are late.
- **Golf scores**: Create a spreadsheet where each player's shots per hole can be entered and which will then produce an overall score per player and a leader board.
- **Weather statistics**: Produce monthly weather statistics for rainfall and temperature using a spreadsheet. Show trends in rainfall and temperatures over a five-year period.

For more ideas have a look through the examples and spreadsheet assignments in *Step by Step Spreadsheets*. The topics listed above are only suggestions and the list of possible spreadsheet projects is endless. What works best is if you can do your spreadsheet project on a topic that interests you, e.g. a hobby or an area that you have worked in before.

FETAC (NCVA) Level 2 Spreadsheet Methods

Sample Exam One

Rapid Repair Services Ltd are involved in the servicing and repair of specialist equipment. They have an expert group of service engineers who travel around the country. Each service engineer is paid travel and overnight expenses. You're required to set up a spreadsheet to calculate the expenses for the engineers. All monetary data should be displayed in currency format with two decimal places.

Table 11.4

	A	B	C	D	E	F
1			Rapid Repair Services Ltd			
2						
3			Travel and Overnight Expenses			
4						
5					Date:	
6						
7	Depart Date	Return Date	Name	Miles	Rate per Mile	Travel Expenses
8	01/05/03	05/05/03	Kelly Miriam	245		
9	04/05/03	06/05/03	Donnelly Helen	76		
10	12/05/03	12/05/03	Murphy James	124		
11	13/05/03	14/05/03	O Brien Mary	65		
12	13/05/03	17/05/03	Regan Thomas	258		
13	14/05/03	14/05/03	Tynan Patrick	158		
14	18/05/03	24/05/03	Dunne Siobhan	248		
15						
16					Total:	
17					Average:	
18						
19	Name:					

1. Set up the spreadsheet and input the data as shown in Table 11.4, with alignments as shown and appropriate column widths.
2. Insert today's date from the computer clock into the cell beside the heading **Date:**
3. Use the IF function to calculate the **rate per mile** based on the following information:

- If the **miles** are less than 100, then the **rate per mile** is €0.60
- If the **miles** are 100 or greater, then the **rate per mile** is €0.50.

4. Calculate the **travel expenses** as the **miles** multiplied by the **rate per mile.**

5. Use the SUM function to calculate the total travel expenses, and display in the cell beside the side heading **Total:**

6. Use the AVERAGE function to calculate the average travel expenses, and display in the cell beside the side heading **Average:**

7. Insert your name in the second column, beside the appropriate label.

8. Save the spreadsheet under the file name **FILE1**, for printing now or later.

9. Produce a printout of the entire spreadsheet **FILE1**, excluding the main heading, and showing row/column identifiers.

10. Produce a printout of the spreadsheet **FILE1** showing all formulas with cell references and row/column identifiers.

11. Delete the record for Thomas Regan from the spreadsheet.

12. Input the additional information as shown in bold print in Table 11.5 on pages 227 and 228, and move the side heading **Date:** and today's date to their new positions.

13. Insert the additional record for Mary Donnelly at the bottom of the list, in the position shown.

14. Delete the contents in the **Rate per Mile** column.

15. Use the Lookup function to insert the rate from the table into the column under the **Rate per Mile** column heading.

16. Use an IF function to calculate the overnight **expenses** based on the following information:

- If the return date is equal to the depart date then there are no overnight expenses.
- If the return date is not equal to the depart date then the overnight expenses are paid at €50.00 per night.

17. Use an IF function to calculate the special expenses based on the following information:

- If the travel expenses are greater than €100.00 and the overnight expenses are € 200.00 or more, then the special expenses are €50.00.
- If the travel expenses are greater than €50.00 and the overnight expenses are €100.00 or more, then the special expenses are €25.00. Otherwise no special expenses are paid.

18. Calculate the **total payment** for each engineer as the sum of **travel expenses, overnight expenses** and **special expenses.**

19. Use the SUM function to calculate the totals for the **travel expenses, overnight expenses, special expenses** and **total payment** columns, and place in the row beside the side heading **Total:** under the appropriate column.

20. Use the AVERAGE function to calculate the average for **travel expenses, overnight expenses, special expenses** and **total payment** and place in the row beside the side heading **Average:** under the appropriate column.

21. Sort the spreadsheet in ascending order on the **Name** column.

22. Save the spreadsheet under the file name **FILE2** for printing now or later.

23. Produce a printout in landscape orientation of the entire spreadsheet **FILE2** showing row/column identifiers.

Table 11.5

	A	B	C	D	E	F	G	H	I	J
1			Rapid Repair Services Ltd							
2										
3			Travel and Overnight Expenses							
4										
5									Date:	
6										
7	Depart Date	Return Date	Name	Miles	Code	Rate per Mile	Travel Expenses	Overnight Expenses	Special Expenses	Total Payment
8	01/05/03	05/05/03	Kelly Miriam	245	A					
9	04/05/03	06/05/03	Donnelly Helen	76	C					
10	12/05/03	12/05/03	Murphy James	124	A					
11	13/05/03	14/05/03	O'Brien Mary	65	B					
12	14/05/03	14/05/03	Tynan Patrick	158	B					
13	18/05/03	24/05/03	Dunne Siobhan	248	C					
14	22/05/03	24/05/03	**Donnelly Mary**	86	C					
15										
16						Total:				

(Contd.)

Table 11.5 (*Contd.*)

	A	B	C	D	E	F	G	H	I	J
17						Average:				
18										
19		Table								
20		Code:	Rate:							
21		A	0.55							
22		B	0.65							
23		C	0.75							
24										
25	Name:									

24. Produce a printout of the spreadsheet **FILE2** showing all formulas with cell references and row/column identifiers.

25. Produce a **column chart** from the spreadsheet **FILE2** to show the total payment paid to each engineer

26. The total payment should be taken from the **Total Payment** column.

27. The column chart should have the heading **Travel and Overnight Payments.**

28. The x axis should have the engineer's name under each bar and have the word **Engineer** as the x axis label.

29. The y axis should show the payment and have the words **Total Payment** as the y axis label.

30. Display the column chart on a separate chart sheet named **CHART.**

31. Print the chart.

Sample Exam Two

Discount Spares Ltd. is a specialist company involved in the production and distribution of spare parts for a limited range of products. You're required to produce a quotation and subsequently convert it into an order and an invoice. Finally, you're required to produce a macro that will clear the invoice.

All monetary data should be displayed in currency format with two decimal places.

Task One

1. Set up the spreadsheet and input the data as shown in Table 11.6 on page 230.

2. The **discount** should be calculated per unit at 10% of the **unit price**.

3. Calculate the **line total** as (the **unit price** minus **discount**) multiplied by the **quantity**.

4. Use the SUM function to calculate the **net** value as the sum of the line totals and display it in the cell beside the side heading **Net**.

5. Calculate the **VAT** at 21% of the net value and display it in the cell beside side heading **VAT**.

6. Calculate the **total** as the **net** plus the **VAT** and display it in the cell beside side heading **Total**.

7. Insert your name and examination number in the second column beside the appropriate labels.

8. Save the spreadsheet under the file name **QUOTE** for printing now or later.

Task Two

1. Input the additional information shown in bold print in Table 11.7 on page 231 and change the second heading in row 3 to Order.

2. Use the lookup function to insert the **type** from the table into the column under the **Type** column heading.

3. Use the **IF** function to display the correct value in the **Disc %** column based on the following information:

- If the **type** is A then the discount is 10%
- If the **type** is B then the discount is 5%
- All other **types** have a 0% discount.

Table 11.6

	A	B	C	D	E	F
1			Discount Spares Ltd			
2						
3			Quotation			
4						
5	Name:	Doyle Bros			Date:	16/05/03
6		Main Street				
7		Dunboyne				
8						
9	Part No.	Description	Qty	Unit Price	Discount	Line Total
10	564	Valve Body	6	56.87		
11	624	Piston	3	36.43		
12	574	Chest Assembly	4	124.67		
13	865	Gasket Set	5	24.32		
14	735	Bolt	25	1.20		
15						
16					Net:	
17					VAT:	
18					Total:	
19						
20	Name:					
21	Exam No:					

Display the figures in the **Disc %** column in percentage format.

4. Delete the values in the discount column and calculate the new **discount** as the disc % multiplied by the **unit price**.

5. Save the spreadsheet under the file name **ORDER** for printing now or later (this printout should be of a selected area, to print the entire spreadsheet but *not* to include the main heading).

Task Three

1. Input the additional information as shown in bold print in Table 11.8 on pages 232 and 233 and change the second heading in row 3 to Invoice. Move side headings as required.

Table 11.7

	A	B	C	D	E	F	G	H
1	Discount Spares Ltd							
2								
3	Order							
4								
5	Name	Doyle Bros					**Order Date:**	16/05/03
6		Main Street						
7		Dunboyne						
8								
9	Part No:	Description	**Type**	Qty	Unit Price	**Disc %**	Discount	Line Total
10	564	Valve Body		6	56.87			
11	624	Piston		3	36.43			
12	574	Chest Assembly		4	124.67			
13	865	Gasket Set		5	24.32			
14	735	Bolt		25	1.20			
15								
16							Net:	
17							VAT:	
18							Total:	
19								
20	**Part No:**	564	574	624	735	865		
21	**Type:**	A	B	A	C	B		
22								
23	Name:							
24	Exam No:							

2. Use the IF function to insert the VAT codes in the **VAT Code** column using the following criteria:

- If the **type** is A then the **VAT code** is 1
- All other **types** have **VAT code** 2.

Table 11.8

	A	B	C	D	E	F	G	H	I	J
1		Discount Spares Ltd								
2										
3					Invoice					
4										
5	Name	Doyle Bros			VAT Code	VAT Rate		Order Date:		16/05/03
6		Main Street			1	21%		Invoice Date:		21/05/03
7		Dunboyne			2	12.5%				
8										
9	Part No:	Description	Type	Qty	Unit Price	Disc %	Discount	VAT Code	VAT Rate	Line Total
10	564	Valve Body		6	56.87					
11	624	Piston		3	36.43					
12	574	Chest Assembly		4	124.67					
13	865	Gasket Set		5	24.32					
14	735	Bolt		25	1.20					
15										
16		Days – Order to Invoice:					Net:			

(Contd.)

Table 11.8 (*Contd.*)

	A	B	C	D	E	F	G	H	I	J
17		Penalty:					VAT:			
18							Total:			
19										
20	Part No:	564	574	624	735	865				
21	Type:	A	B	A	C	B				
22										
23	Name:									
24	Exam No:									

3. Use the lookup function to insert the correct **VAT rate** into the column under the **VAT Rate** column heading.

4. Display the **VAT rate** in percentage format with one decimal place.

5. Use a formula to calculate the number of days between the **order date** and the **invoice date** using the dates on the invoice and place in the cell beside the **Days – Order to Invoice:** side heading.

6. Calculate the penalty using the **Days – Order to Invoice** value and place in the cell beside the side heading **Penalty**. The calculation should be based on the following criteria:

- If the number of days is five or more then the penalty is 2% of the total
- If the number of days is three or four then the penalty is 1% of the total
- If the number of days is less than three there is no penalty.

7. Display the penalty in currency format (no decimal places).

8. Recalculate the **VAT** using the appropriate **VAT rates** and **line totals**.

9. Sort the spreadsheet in ascending order on the **description** column.

10. Save the spreadsheet under the file name **INVOICE** for printing now or later. Produce two printouts, in landscape orientation, of INVOICE to show (i) **values** and (ii) **formulas** and **cell references**.

Task Four

1. Produce a **macro** that will perform the following tasks on **INVOICE**. (**Note:** Ensure that you save the file INVOICE **before** producing or testing the macro and don't run/execute the macro on INVOICE.)

2. Delete the order date and the invoice date.

3. Delete the name and address.

4. Delete the values from the **Part Number** and **Description** columns.

5. Delete the values from the **Quantity** and **Unit Price** columns.

6. Insert the date from the computer clock in cell headed **Invoice Date**.

7. Save the macro under the name **CLEAR** (either separately or as part of the spreadsheet INVOICE) for printing now or later.

Glossary of Spreadsheet Terms

Absolute Cell Reference

An absolute cell reference may be used in a formula or a function. Absolute cell references don't change when the formula or function is moved or copied. A cell reference can be made absolute by inserting $ on either side of the reference to the column letter. Example: A1 is relative, $A$1 is absolute.

Cell Name

A name can be assigned to an individual cell by selecting the cell and then entering a name in the name box, which is part of the formula bar. Once a cell has been given a name this name can be used in formulas, e.g. =B2*taxrate. Cell names are absolute.

Chart

A method of representing data graphically so that trends and exceptional values can be quickly recognised. In a chart numbers can be represented by vertical columns, horizontal bars, slices of a pie or dots that are joined up to form a line.

Chart Sheet

A sheet within a workbook that displays a chart separate from the data on which the chart is based.

Condition

A test carried out by an IF function using a logical operator.

Conditional Formatting

A method of emphasising particular cells in a range of cells. Formatting can be applied to cells that match a certain condition or multiple conditions. For example, amounts that are greater than €100 could be displayed in red.

Custom Sort

A custom sort can be used where the required order doesn't follow an alphabetical pattern. For example, if weekdays were sorted alphabetically the result would be Friday, Monday, Saturday, Sunday, Thursday, Tuesday, Wednesday. A custom sort is required to display days in sequential order (Monday, Tuesday, Wednesday, Thursday, Friday, Saturday, Sunday).

False Action

The section of an IF function that's implemented when the condition isn't satisfied.

Formatting Toolbar

A toolbar containing buttons that, when clicked, will change the appearance of the current cell or range of cells. In the formatting toolbar you can select the font style and size; change the text to bold, italics or underline; align the contents of a cell or range of cells to the left, right or centre; select a format for numbers; change the number of decimal places; and select font and background colours.

Formula

A method of calculation using a combination of cell references together with the arithmetic operators + - * /. Brackets may be used to change the natural order of calculation in a formula. In any formula that doesn't contain brackets, multiplication and division are always done first. The exponential symbol (^) may be used to raise a number to a power in a formula.

Formula Bar

This appears above the column headings. It displays the cell reference of the current location of the cell pointer. It also displays the contents of the current cell, which may be a number, text, a formula or a function.

Function

A method of calculation by referring to a function name and a range of cells, e.g. =max(A2:A10). Each function is set up to carry out a number of tasks. Using functions can reduce the amount of calculations carried out by the spreadsheet user.

Logical Operator

Logical operators are used in the condition of an IF function. They are also used in AND functions and OR functions. They are combined with cell references, values and/or text to form logical expressions.

Table 1

Logical Operator	Meaning
=	Equal to
<	Less than
<=	Less than or equal to
>	Greater than
>=	Greater than or equal to
<>	Not equal to

Lookup Table

A lookup table stores data that can be referenced by a lookup function. Lookup tables are very useful where there's a large amount of data to be referenced. For example, a lookup table could store all the bar codes, product descriptions and prices of products in a hardware store.

Macro

A method of automating repetitive spreadsheet tasks. A series of spreadsheet commands are recorded and stored in the macro. When the macro is played back, all of the recorded commands are executed at high speed.

Paste Special

This can be used to copy a value from a single cell or range of cells and then use this value or values to update data stored in another cell or range of cells using addition, subtraction, multiplication or division.

Pivot Chart

A method of graphically representing data stored in a pivot table. If the pivot table changes when it's refreshed, these changes are automatically incorporated in the pivot chart.

Pivot Table

A table that allows data to be categorised and summarised. A pivot table can analyse a list of data by calculating sub-totals for items that appear more than once in a particular column. The effects of adding new data to the list can be seen by refreshing the pivot table.

Protect Sheet

A method of restricting access to cells within a worksheet. When a worksheet is protected, data can only be entered in cells that have been unlocked by the spreadsheet designer.

Protect Workbook

Protecting a workbook prevents people from deleting, moving or renaming worksheets contained in the workbook.

Range

Two or more cells in a spreadsheet that can be highlighted either by clicking and dragging with the mouse, holding down the shift key and pressing an arrow key or by pressing F8 followed by an arrow key. Multiple ranges can be highlighted by holding down the CTRL key as you highlight cells.

Range Name

A name can be assigned to a range of cells by highlighting the cells and then entering a name in the name box, which is part of the formula bar. Once a range has been given a name, this name can be used in functions, e.g. =sum(sales).

Relative Cell Reference

A relative cell reference may be used in a formula or a function. Relative cell references change when the formula or function is moved or copied depending on the direction in which the formula or function is moved or copied.

Sort

Data stored in a spreadsheet can be rearranged into ascending or descending alphabetical or numerical order by clicking the Sort Ascending or Sort Descending button.

Spreadsheet Window

This is the section of the spreadsheet that you can see on the screen at any given time.

Standard Toolbar

A toolbar that contains buttons for opening and saving workbooks, printing, moving and copying, sorting, creating charts and getting help from Excel. Each button on the toolbar represents a command that may be accessed through the menu. For example, clicking the Save button is the same as selecting File followed by Save.

True Action

The section of an IF function that's implemented when the condition is satisfied.

Workbook

A collection of worksheets that are saved as part of one spreadsheet file.

Worksheet

An individual sheet in a workbook. Each workbook can have anywhere between one and 255 worksheets. Worksheets can be linked using formulas.

Worksheet Tabs

The worksheet tabs display the names of the sheets in the workbook. Each worksheet can be displayed by clicking its worksheet tab.